P9-CCS-075

SOUNDS LIKE TITANIC

SOUNDS
LIKE
TITANIC

A Memoir

Jessica
Chiccehitto
Hindman

W. W. NORTON & COMPANY
INDEPENDENT PUBLISHERS SINCE 1923
NEW YORK LONDON

Sounds Like Titanic is a work of nonfiction. Names and potentially identifying features of individuals, as well as minor details of chronology, have been changed, and dialogue has been reconstructed.

For information about permission to reproduce selections from this book, write to Permissions, W. W. Norton & Company, Inc., 500 Fifth Avenue, New York, NY 10110

For information about special discounts for bulk purchases, please contact W. W. Norton Special Sales at specialsales@wwnorton.com or 800-233-4830

Manufacturing by LSC Communications, Harrisonburg
Book design by Daniel Lagin
Production manager: Lauren Abbate

ISBN 978-0-393-65164-5

W. W. Norton & Company, Inc., 500 Fifth Avenue, New York, N.Y. 10110
www.wwnorton.com

W. W. Norton & Company Ltd., 15 Carlisle Street, London W1D 3BS

1 2 3 4 5 6 7 8 9 0

To those with average talents and above-average desires.

It was as though the scene through which I had just lived had been a monstrous and comic miming for ends I could not conceive and for an audience I could not see but which I knew was leering from the shadow.

—Robert Penn Warren, *All the King's Men*

Contents

A Note on This Book

This is a memoir about working as a fake violinist for a famous American composer, referred to in this book as The Composer. While this is a memoir about being a fake, this is not a fake memoir. This is a memoir in earnest, written by a person striving to get at the truth of things that happened in her past.

On the other hand, there is a kind of sleight of hand necessarily involved in all writing, especially personal narrative. The idea that the word "I" can function as a static entity on the page—instead of a shape-shifting representation of an actual human being who changes her mind, sometimes on a moment-to-moment basis, about everything from what she wants for lunch to what her place is in the universe—is perhaps the biggest fakery of all. It is my belief that the first years of the twenty-first century were boom times for all kinds of fakery, perhaps because suddenly reality didn't seem very real anymore, and everyone got confused. In the 2000s reality became "reality." Television critics scoffed at "reality" television, because it wasn't real, while Karl Rove mocked actual reality (and the "reality-based community") as a pointless annoyance for people running an empire. America had become so powerful, Rove suggested, that we could make our own facts, like we make our own hamburgers.

But the difference between the real and the fake does, in fact, matter. This book argues that while determining the difference between the real and the fake can be maddening and ultimately imperfect, it remains a worthy endeavor. (Even if, in some cases, including my own, faking is needed to discover what is real.) As an active member of the reality-based community, I would like to state that even though I have changed the names and identifying features of characters in this book, have consolidated some conversations with multiple people into single conversations with one person, and have fake-fiddled with minor points of chronology, identifying biographical details and quotations from people like fans—and even though other musicians who worked with The Composer may have different experiences, memories, and perspectives—all of the events chronicled here, to the best of my knowledge and memory, are true.

SOUNDS LIKE TITANIC

PART I
Departures

We live in a nation whose every other impulse is theatrical, but whose every other impulse is to insist upon "authenticity."

—Richard Rodriguez,
Brown: The Last Discovery of America

How to Become a Famous Violinist

The space between a violin's fingerboard and its bridge is about an inch wide. If a bead of sweat from the right hand causes the bow to slip a millimeter to the right or left, the horsehair will crash against the bridge or screech across the fingerboard. The left hand navigates an even narrower plank, approaching the fingerboard at an unnatural angle, with no spatial clues to guide fingers into their correct positions. Pianos, winds, percussion—they have keys waiting to be hit. But to produce a pure sound on a violin is to search for it in a haystack of squeaks, scratches, and sour notes.

Violinists perform with a ferocious physicality that's easy to mock: bow hairs break, brows furrow, torsos and legs contort into bizarre poses. Some violinists, like Nadja Salerno-Sonnenberg, talk to the instrument as they play. Others, like Joshua Bell, slash the instrument as if in battle. Still others seduce it, their fingers encircling, caressing the instrument's neck. Regardless of the approach, the violinist must hurry each note through a narrow keyhole of time; sustaining sound is a race against the finite length of the bow.

Many people believe there is only one path to becoming a famous violinist. I am here to report that there are actually two.

WAYS TO BECOME A FAMOUS VIOLINIST: A COMPREHENSIVE LIST

By: Jessica Chiccehitto Hindman, Famous Violinist

Option #1: Be born with prodigious musical talent in or near a city with an excellent music conservatory, such as New York or Moscow or London. Begin lessons early and develop your gift by practicing the violin for at least two to four hours each day under the supervision of a skilled maestro. Win acceptance to a world-class conservatory and practice for at least six to eight hours each day. In a series of hundreds of grueling auditions, master classes, and recitals, beat out hundreds of other violinists. Begin solo career. Be better than the handful of other violinists with major solo careers so they don't muscle you out of lucrative performances and recording contracts. Continue to practice at an exhausting pace for the rest of your life and/or until your fingers snarl into an arthritic tangle and/or until one day, undone by the pressure of being one of the top musicians in the world, you (a) collapse into a pile of neurotic mush; or (b) begin passive-aggressively pursuing hobbies that conflict with your career as a violinist, such as lumber splitting or knife juggling or sword-smithing; or (c) retire to a life of teaching "Twinkle, Twinkle, Little Star" to the young children of hedge fund managers.

Option #2: Play very softly in front of a dead microphone while a CD recording of another more talented violinist is blasted toward an unknowing audience. Go on a fifty-four-city tour of America doing this. Go on a six-city tour of China doing this. Appear on national television broadcasts narrated by Hollywood celebrities doing this. Land gigs at Carnegie Hall and Lincoln Center doing this. Pay your college tuition and New York City rent doing this.

Notice that even though the music the audience hears is not being produced by you, the audience's applause for you, their praise, their standing ovations, are real.

Notice that the inability to distinguish Option #1 from Option #2, the inability to distinguish real from fake, is a classic sign of mental illness.

God Bless America Tour 2004
New York City to Philadelphia

The Composer is broiling himself a cake. None of us— Harriet, Stephen, Patrick, or me—know it is his birthday until he begins mixing batter while our RV inches through traffic in the bowels of the Lincoln Tunnel. The oven isn't working, so The Composer holds the cake under the broiler's pilot light. The cabin fills with the smell of oven gas. A pinpoint of light appears in the tunnel and we emerge into the sun-cooked marshes of industrial New Jersey, the entire North American continent spread before us, the Manhattan skyline receding in the rearview mirror.

A few feet from where The Composer kneels at the oven, I sit in the RV's dining booth, looking at the tour schedule. It is a bound and laminated book with "God Bless America Tour, August–November, 2004" written on the title page. It is Tour Day One: New York City to Philadelphia. We have 74 days and 54 performances to go before we return to New York City, where we will perform our final concert to a sold-out audience at Carnegie Hall.

After an hour of kneeling by the broiler, The Composer places the still-liquid cake on the stovetop and spoons on dollops of Cool Whip before arranging whole strawberries on top. While his back is turned, the RV hits a bump in the road and the cake flies off the stovetop, through the air, across the RV, and directly into the trash can by the door. Berry-whipped carnage covers the cabinets, the floor, the sides of the trash can. The Composer retreats to his bedroom in the back of the RV and closes the door behind him.

I open the small, cake-splattered kitchen cubby assigned to me. Inside are books that seemed appropriate to bring on a three-month tour across America with The Composer: Kerouac's *On the Road*, Steinbeck's *Travels with Charley*, Twain's *Roughing It*, Robert Penn Warren's *All the King's Men*, Austen's *Pride and Prejudice*, Nabokov's *Lolita*, and Azar Nafisi's *Reading Lolita in Tehran*. But instead of a book I take out my journal. Even though the ride is so bumpy I can barely keep the tip of my pen on the paper, I begin to write.

There is something about The Composer that I need to know, but I'm not sure what it is.

I look around at the cake-smeared cabin. The Composer is someone who will bake himself a birthday cake in a moving vehicle, with a broken oven, in front of four employees who believe he is doomed to failure, if not death by fiery explosion. The fact that the cake had no chance didn't stop him from trying to bake it.

It will be a long time before I understand anything much about what I write in that journal. Many years later, thinking back on this moment, I come across an article asking why so many memoirists are writing in the second person these days. The prevailing theory is that memoirists use second person when they are writing about something traumatic. But I have an additional theory: For many people, myself included, sitting down to write something in the first person feels like the worst type of fakery. There is no way "I" am in front of the live microphone, no way anyone would want to listen to "me," no way anyone has paid to attend this concert starring "myself," and so I become "you," and in faking you, I am finally able to say what I want to say.

New York City
1999

You spend your first night in New York City in Penn Station with an elderly homeless woman named Rose. She eyes you from across the station—an eighteen-year-old girl wearing khakis and a white t-shirt from the Gap, sprawled on the floor between a bare-breasted goddess mural and a McDonalds, pretending to read *The Iliad*—and decides you are in over your head.

It is almost two in the morning and the rust-colored concourse is suddenly empty. There is a calamitous noise as the food vendors unroll the floor-to-ceiling security cages in front of their darkened shops. But then the pretzel-scented air falls still, and where thousands of people walked just a few hours before, the footsteps of a single person can now be heard from a long distance.

Unlike the other names of places on the subway map—125th Street, 72nd Street, Columbus Circle—Penn Station suggests something familiar: a station! Having nowhere else to go for the night, knowing no one in the entire city of eight million people, and not daring to call your parents, you choose Penn Station because you have vague recollections from movies of a beautiful train station in New York City where men in business suits hurry along marble corridors underneath a chapel-like, star-painted ceiling. Penn Station, you think, will be a reasonable place to spend the night. You have yet to learn that even in New York City men in business suits go home after a certain hour. You have yet to learn that in the dead of night, another, slower-moving civilization—the city's homeless, many suffering from mental illness—pace the station's dingy, labyrinthine corridors. You have yet to learn that the beautiful train station in the movies is Grand Central, and that Penn Station has all the charm of a crime scene.

Rose sidles up to you, asking if you have missed your train. She appears to be in her sixties or seventies and wears her graying hair in a tight, greasy bun. Her t-shirt and jeans are worn and she carries a large grocery bag brimming with clothing and household items. You aren't waiting for a train, you say, you are spending the night. She tells you that you should come sit with her in the passenger waiting area. But the sign says it's for ticketed Amtrak passengers. You don't want to get into trouble. Rose points out that you'll get into plenty more trouble once the group of men lingering around a nearby trash can notices you are alone. Okay, you say. And so you sit with Rose in the Amtrak waiting area, and she teaches you how to tie your suitcase to your leg with a plastic bag so it won't get stolen if you fall asleep.

You are spending the night in Penn Station because you have
gone AWOL from the Air Force. Eighteen hours before Rose introduces herself to you in Penn Station, you took a plane then a bus and
then a subway and then walked to Manhattan College (located in
the Bronx) where you changed into an ROTC uniform and followed
a drill sergeant into the swampy mid-August heat to run laps around
a glass-strewn track. In those few hours you completed many push-
ups for your country.

After an hour of exercise in the muggy Bronx air, you and the
other recruits are marched into a lecture room where you listen to
a presentation about the U.S. Air Force winning the war in Kosovo.
"We killed everyone we needed to kill from the air," the drill sergeant says, as if this fact should fill you with pride, instead of surprise. You've never heard someone brag about killing people before.
He adds that the era of "real wars" is over, but the Air Force will still
be the first to respond if the United States needs to "bomb someone."

After the lecture you are marched outside for an orientation session.
You sit with a small group of your fellow ROTC recruits on a grassy
hill. The sergeant asks everyone to go around the circle: State your
name, where you will be attending college, and what you'll be studying.

*Hi, I'm Marcus, and I'll be a freshman at the Queens School of Aero-
nautics where I'm going to study aviation and I want to be a pilot . . .*

*Hi, I'm Javier, and I'll be a freshman at the Queens School of Aero-
nautics where I'm going to study aviation and engineering so I can be a
pilot or an engineer . . .*

*Hi, I'm Tyrell, and I'll be a freshman at the Queens School of
Aeronautics . . .*

*Hi, I'm Jessica, and in a few weeks I'll be a freshman at Columbia
University where I'm planning to major in music—I play the violin! My*

parents can't pay the tuition, so, uh, here I am! If music doesn't work out, maybe I'll major in anthropology or history . . . maybe art history! I have a lot of interests! Apart from a violinist, I'd like to be a journalist, but apparently Columbia thinks journalism is vocational, so, you know, I can't major in it. But maybe music will work out . . . um, so, yeah, that's me! Hi! Thanks!

It is the first time you have ever introduced yourself as a music major, and in saying it out loud it now occurs to you that it is true. This isn't some faraway dream. You are eighteen years old and have arrived in the big city, THE big city, to study music. And as you listen to the other kids talk about their life goals, you realize something else: You are someone whose upbringing was upper class enough to make you believe you could make music for a living, but lower class enough to provide no knowledge of how to do it. As for the money, your parents abide by the prevailing cultural notions of rural Appalachia, where you grew up: Any tuition shortfall can be remedied by signing up for the military.

Later that night—your first in the city where you will live for the next ten years but one that you have no idea how to navigate—as you wonder where you will sleep (Penn Station sounds like a safe bet!) and how many subway tokens it will take to get there, you write a note to your drill sergeant:

Dear Drill Sergeant,

I have decided that ROTC is not for me. My mom made me sign up to pay for college, but I never wanted to do this. I want to be a violinist, and though I know very little about the Air Force (as you could probably tell!), I'm pretty sure there isn't a great need for string players. As a patriotic American, believe me when I tell you I am doing my country a service by quitting.

Sincerely,
Jessica Chiccehitto Hindman

PS: I am eighteen years old—a legal adult. Please do not contact my parents.

You leave the note on the desk in the dormitory room you'd been assigned a few hours earlier, your ROTC uniform folded on the bed. Carrying your suitcase in both arms so it won't make noise on the floor, you sneak past a security guard and out a side door that opens onto a dark alley. Once you are a block away, you set down your suitcase and race into the hot Bronx night.

God Bless America Tour 2004
Philadelphia

ACT I: WHAT IS UNSEEN

The Composer runs laps around the PBS station parking lot. He wears his concert clothes—black pants, blue dress shirt—and his running shoes. Harriet, Stephen, and I watch him from inside the RV, where we change into our concert clothes while dancing to Out-Kast. When he finishes his run, The Composer asks us to come outside, where Patrick is unloading the sound equipment for our first concert on the God Bless America Tour. Patrick is a retired union contract negotiator who loves The Composer's music so much that he has negotiated himself into a contract to drive the The Composer's Ensemble across America for no money. He has never driven an RV before but seems content in his role, so long as he can listen to The Composer's music while driving.

Harriet, Stephen, and I file out of the air-conditioned RV onto the sticky asphalt. Stephen, a flutist, wears an all-black suit and tie. A tall, thin, bespectacled man in his midthirties, Stephen has one of those kind, encouraging faces that induces calm in others. Harriet and I wear long black dresses with stockings and heels. Harriet is in her early thirties but looks much younger. She has short black hair that emphasizes her high cheekbones and big brown eyes. She's tall and beautiful in a flawless, preppy way, like a J. Crew model, and also plays violin. I stand beside her, a much shorter, twenty-three-year-old woman, my rhinestone concert barrettes restraining waves of long, thick, unruly black hair.

"Hey, um, you guys, could you give us a hand?" The Composer asks.

The Composer refers to us as "you guys" because, despite the fact that I have worked for him for over two years, despite the fact that he is supposed to announce my name at every concert on the God Bless America Tour for the next three months, he still does not know that my name is Jessica. When he needs my attention, he calls me Melissa.

His request for manual labor floats thick on the hot August air, blending with the noxious fumes from the RV's exhaust pipe and the faint scent of ruined birthday cake. I look at Harriet, who looks at Stephen. Without saying anything, we understand. The Composer can replace us with musicians who are even more desperate for work than we are—new immigrants from Russia, Hungary, Romania, China. The world is full of starving musicians.

Harriet picks up a heavy, dusty bag full of extension cords. Stephen helps Patrick lift a film projector, and The Composer deadlifts an amplifier. I lug a cardboard box full of The Composer's CDs and stumble under the weight of it, teetering in my concert heels. We make several trips back and forth from the RV to the concert room. By the time we are finished, our concert clothes are smeared with sweat and sawdust. My feet are bleeding from lifting boxes in high-heeled shoes, but my concert dress is long enough to hide the damage.

ACT II: WHAT IS UNHEARD

The Composer enters stage left, bouncing toward his electric piano with childlike exuberance, waving and beaming at the cheering audience. Two violinists and a flutist follow him onto the stage. He sits down at his piano while his musicians stand behind three microphones. Without pausing to tune, they lift their instruments and begin. Two film projection screens on either side of the stage light up with images of an eagle swooping over the Grand Canyon.

The audience hears the soaring sound of a pennywhistle—a recorder-like flute that produces the high-pitched wail made famous by Céline Dion's ballad "My Heart Will Go On" from the film *Titanic*. The audience also hears the sounds of the violins and piano. But no one except the three musicians can see The Composer press the Play button on a portable Sony CD player he bought that morning at a Walmart for $14.95.

ACT III: WHAT IS UNNOTICED

Halfway through the concert The Composer introduces us to the crowd. He says, "The woman here with the biggest, most beautiful smile is Harriet. Doesn't she have the biggest smile? Give her a hand!"

Then he gestures to me and says, "This is . . . uh . . . Melissa! Melissa on the violin, everybody! Isn't she great? Give her a hand!"

Audition

New York City, 2002

"**I**s this Jessica? Jessica, the violinist?" The voice on your dorm telephone is Becca Belge, assistant manager of the The Composer's Ensemble. Can you come to the office for an interview? Yes. Can you come right now? Yes.

The office is a few blocks away and you race down Broadway in what you consider to be your most job-interview-worthy outfit, a red-sequined blouse and white skirt, your violin case strapped to your back.

You have been working two jobs that summer in the never-ending quest to pay your college tuition, but you are coming up short. It is already June and you have less than two months to come up with $8,000 for the fall semester of your senior year. So each night, after working at your second job, you have taken the subway home, eaten a $2 slice of Sicilian pizza, and searched the Internet for a third. And each night you have noticed there are very few well-paying jobs available for twenty-one-year-old college students that do not involve sex work.

But then you came across a posting on a student LISTSERV:

Seeking violinists and flute players to perform in award-winning ensemble that has performed on PBS and NPR and at Lincoln Center. Must be able to work every Friday, Saturday, and Sunday. $150/day with potential bonuses. Send résumé and demo tape to Becca Belge, Assistant Production Manager.

You had never seen an advertisement like this. Professional ensembles, whether classical, folk, or punk rock, do not place advertisements on college LISTSERVs, and they hire by audition, not by an open call for demo tapes.

You read the ad again and again. If you got this job, you would double your current income. More than that, you would become what you had spent your childhood dreaming of becoming: a professional violinist.

One problem: You aren't very good at playing the violin. You dropped your music major shortly after arriving at college. Your freshman dormitory alone housed dozens of better-than-you violinists. Looking at the strange job ad, you began calculating how many better-than-you violinists might exist on the Upper West Side (hundreds), in Manhattan (thousands), and all of New York City (millions?!).

Still, you decided to try, enlisting a friend who worked at the student radio station to help you record a demo tape. Before the recording session, you practiced for hours. You planned and replanned which pieces to include on the tape and in which order—fast tempo, slow tempo, fast tempo; Bach, Corelli, Mozart; technical, expressive, technical; a piece to showcase the fingers, a piece to showcase the bow, a piece to showcase the vibrato. You revised your résumé to make yourself seem more musical. You dropped your application into a mailbox, thinking to yourself: *At least you tried.*

Three days later, Becca Belge hustles you into a dark two-bedroom apartment full of dumpy-looking office furniture. Stacks of CDs teeter on top of the stove's burners, microphone cords snake around the kitchen floor, piles of sheet music overflow from the windowsills.

Becca is a tall, round woman with red hair and a red face. She wears a t-shirt, denim skirt, and plastic flip-flops. She offers you a metal folding chair and you say, *Thank you, Ms. Belge*, and she booms *Call me Becca* while ransacking a file cabinet, flinging sheet music onto the floor. You sit on the folding chair with your violin case in your lap and attempt to steal glances at the sheet music. At any moment Becca will ask you to sight-read it, and you know that your lack of sight-reading skills will doom this audition, will separate you—the hardworking but untalented person who mailed in an acceptable demo tape—from the job applicant who is gifted, the prodigy who can perform any musical score at first glance.

"Here it is," Becca says, holding out a sheet of paper.

What is it? Some impossible Dvořák concerto? A finger-twisting Kreutzer étude? A Bach partita that will make your chin crunch into your violin while you saw and scratch and reveal yourself to be an amateur posing as the real thing?

But it isn't sheet music. It's a W-4 tax form.

You've had enough jobs to know that filling out a W-4 means you are hired. But how can you be hired? You haven't played anything. You haven't even been interviewed. Becca isn't asking you any questions. She is telling you to complete the W-4 and you are nodding and filling it out and she is asking if you have plans for the weekend.

"Because if you don't," she says, "we need you to go to New Hampshire."

"Okay," you say, as if going to New Hampshire is something you do all the time. You've been north of New York City once, for a night visiting a friend in Boston. *New Hampshire?*

"New Hampshire!" Becca is saying, adding something about Yevgeny, a Russian violinist who is to meet you on a Manhattan street corner on Thursday night. He will drive you to New Hampshire where you will meet up with Debbie, a flute player. The trip to New Hampshire will be your "training weekend," and it will be your job to sell CDs during the live concert.

"So, should I bring my violin?" you ask, confused.

"You probably won't need it, and there won't be much space in Yevgeny's car," Becca replies. "But if all goes well with the training," she assures you, "you will work as a violinist the following weekend."

Becca hands you a stack of sheet music and nine CDs. The CD jackets feature bucolic scenes—a blossoming tree, a lighthouse, a meadow by a stream. Written across the top of every CD cover is the name of The Composer.

"Who is he?" you ask.

She gestures to the CDs. "This is all his music."

You have never heard of The Composer, but you don't say anything to Becca. Instead you make a face like, "Ah, yes, of course! The legendary Composer!" Three years at college have taught you to avoid being, in the words of one future Rhodes Scholar and congressman, "that twit with the Southern accent." Since then you've discovered that, thanks to the Internet, even a twit with a Southern accent can learn what she needs to get by.

Who Is The Composer?

Who hat the Internet says:

W The Composer has sold millions of albums. His benefit albums for charity have reached No. 1 on the Classical Billboard chart. Hollywood A-list celebrities narrate his PBS specials, which have raised millions of dollars for public television. His conducting credits include the most prestigious orchestras in the United States and the world.

He has performed with orphans in Africa and was sponsored by the U.S. State Department to spread goodwill in communist countries. He provides free CDs to American soldiers in the Middle East. His compositions stream through hospital speakers across America and are thought by many to have curative properties.

In less than fifteen years, The Composer has released over thirty albums of his compositions. He regularly appears live on the QVC shopping channel, where his albums sell by the thousands per minute. Purchasers of his CDs leave orgasmic online reviews like "my heart is tingling," "the world's most beautiful music," and "this music is my personal opiate."

God Bless America Tour 2004
Philadelphia to Atlanta

The Composer spends most of his time in the back bedroom of the RV, composing. He has few reasons to emerge, for everything he needs is on top of his bed: a full-size keyboard, folding chair, two bookcase-length plywood boards, a dozen stuffed animals, enough dusty concert wires to amp the New York Philharmonic, a film projector, half-empty boxes of Cap'n Crunch, a crate of apples, a pungent pile of running clothes. While the rest of us sleep in hotel rooms, The Composer sleeps in the RV every night, presumably on top of the keyboard.

Per The Composer's orders, one of us—me, Harriet, Stephen, or The Composer himself—rides in the passenger seat with Patrick at all times in order to help him navigate and to DJ Patrick's favorite road tunes on the RV's sound system. His favorite road tunes, Patrick insists, are all of The Composer's albums. As official Ensemble musicians, The Composer's employees, and people spending most of our waking hours with The Composer, objecting to Patrick's choice of music has obvious perils. Then comes our first thirteen-hour day on the road and Harriet (passive), Stephen (avoids confrontation), and I (wimp) threaten bloody mutiny if we have to listen to another goddamned note. The Composer stays mum on the issue, but I suspect that even he doesn't want to listen to his music any more than he has to.

Of all of us, Harriet has the best taste in music. When not on tour, she lives in Chicago, where she plays in symphony orchestras during the day, swanky clubs at night. She has rare demo recordings of Chicago musicians who went on to be famous. Everyone wants to hire Harriet as a violinist. She's gorgeous yet old-fashioned, the sort of person who punctuates her speech with phrases like "Bless your soul" while flashing a killer smile. She's agreed to the God Bless America Tour because she wanted to get away from a complicated situation with a man back home. It felt like the right time to go on a road trip.

Thirteen hours in an RV is a lot of time to listen to music. As the RV barrels south into the hot yellow light of late August, we listen to country, rap, hip-hop, bluegrass, classical, jazz, classic rock, gospel, grunge, Broadway, indie, and blues. The trees get taller and leafier, the cornstalks higher. The soil turns blood red and we are in Georgia.

Somewhere in rural northern Georgia, I decide to play the first movement of Beethoven's Fifth Symphony. The moment I push the Play button I hear The Composer flailing his way up the cabin toward us. He perches in the space between Patrick and me, listening to the music, the infamous swelling variations on da da da *dah*—perhaps the four most recognizable notes in human history.

And then, The Composer asks me a question that—had it come from any other musician, let alone a Billboard-topping classical composer who has performed with the New York Philharmonic—I would have taken as a joke. But The Composer is sincere, speaking in the friendly just-making-obligatory-chit-chat-with-the-help voice he uses with me, the person whose name he thinks is Melissa.

"I like this music," he says of the opening to Beethoven's Fifth Symphony. "What is it?"

Imposter Syndrome

After your interview with Becca, you float up July-drenched Broadway back to your dorm, past the roasted-nut vendors, the incense peddlers, the sidewalk displays of used books for sale, the lone saxophonist outside the West End bar who plays the theme to *Sesame Street* over and over again. *Sunny days . . .* You clutch your sheet music and CDs, their plastic covers sweating in the heat.

You have gotten the job. A violin job! You feel like a violinist in a way that you never have before, despite thirteen years of practice, lessons, and school performances. All of your years of practicing are going to "pay off," that distinctively American phrase that conflates all work with reward, all positive outcomes with money.

But it isn't just the money. You can tell your parents, your high school teachers, and all of the adults in your rural hometown who supported you—from setting up the folding chairs at high school concerts to driving you to auditions to sending you cards of encouragement (one from your eighth-grade science teacher: *You have a real gift! We are all so proud of you! Never stop practicing!*)—that all of their hard work, and all of yours, will amount to something. It doesn't matter that you weren't born a prodigy. It doesn't matter that you aren't as good as the other violinists at Columbia. It doesn't matter that while those kids were taking lessons at Julliard and giving concerts at Carnegie Hall, you were performing solos in your school's "auditorium," which was also your school's cafeteria and gym, the nearest real auditorium hours away over the mountaintops.

None of that matters because you have worked hard and "made it," another distinctive American phrase. *And, If I can make it there, I'll make it anywhere . . .* Years later you will question the way this phrase has warped your consciousness. You will discover that "make it," as an expression, emerged in the American vernacular during the Gilded Age. The wealth disparities of that era are reflected in "make it," which evolved to mean both mere survival (*make it through the winter*) and wild success involving money, fame, and/or acclaim (*make it big*), forever linking these two vastly different outcomes in the American mind.

But for now you simply think to yourself that you have "made it." You are the kid from the rural South—Appalachia no less!—that twit with the Southern accent. Who has Beat The Odds. *Start spreadin' the news* . . . You are it. You are proof. The real deal. (The money!) You are a professional classical violinist in New York City.

Then you think *No, this can't be right. You aren't good enough to be a professional classical violinist in New York City. There has been some horrible mistake.*

West Virginia
1985

The movie *Sarah and the Squirrel* is not about a girl having some carefree fun with her critter pal, as one might expect from the cartoon picture of a girl and a squirrel—both smiling—on the VHS case. Within the first few minutes of the video, Sarah's village is invaded by Nazis, her family members captured and taken to a concentration camp. Sarah escapes the slaughter by hiding in an adjacent forest. It is under these circumstances of genocide, starvation, and exposure to the elements that she befriends (or perhaps hallucinates) a squirrel. In the cartoon's last frame, Sarah wanders alone and barefoot through the snow. All of these events are set to violin music.

You are four years old and watching the movie alone in the golden-hued living room of your family's small, rented house. Your dad joins you on the foam couch for the last few minutes of the movie, just as the violin music reaches peak crescendo and Sarah's fate as a Holocaust victim becomes clear. He begins to sputter explanations about bad people, good people, Anne Frank, sometimes people die, Jews, wars . . .

"What's the music?" you ask.

"Violin music," he replies, elated at the change in subject. "Maybe it was Brahms!"

Your Dad was no classical music expert; he didn't know Brahms from a wild turkey. He did know how to play three chords on the living room piano, an instrument utilized only by him, and then only as an alarm clock: "It's time to wake uuuuuup!" he'd sing in a gleeful fake baritone on mornings before school or church, banging out his three known chords while you and your brothers remained in bed, giggling. "Why is no-bod-eee uuuuuuup!" But as this was the extent of his musical repertoire, you assume he got the name "Brahms" from one of those mail-order cassette tape compilations so popular in the 1980s—*All the masterpieces of classical music in one box!*

You tell him you want to play the Brahms. You figure "the Brahms" must be something like the drums, but played on a violin.

"And that's when Jessica said she wanted to play Brahms," is how he told the story for years afterward, as if you had pulled the name of a nineteenth-century German composer out of your head at four years old.

Decades later, while working as a professional violinist for The Composer, you notice that parents of children who play instruments love to share early-musical-interest-origin stories, regardless of the child's actual talent (or lack thereof). Such parents recite their child's first response to music as if it were a holy event, like the moment in a hagiography when a saint first hears God: *My son would bang on pots and pans. My daughter would bang on the piano. Before he could walk. Before she could talk. He would sing in the bath. She would sing in her*

*crib. He'd smile when I played a Mozart record. Her face would light up
at the sound of Beethoven.*

Your dad told the Brahms story in a similar fashion, as if it was
proof, or maybe reassurance, that you were destined for greatness.

The Nose-Picking Section
New York City, 2002

After your interview with Becca, you realize that you must face
two conflicting facts:

1. You have been hired to play violin for a famous composer who
   performs with the New York Philharmonic at Lincoln Center.
2. You lack the skills to play violin at that level. It would take
   you at least a decade of nonstop lessons and practice to even
   approach that level of performance. But you don't have a
   decade. You have two days.

In the face of these truths, you do the only thing you can think of to
do: You take out your violin and begin to practice.

The first thing you notice as you sight-read The Composer's
compositions is their rhythmic simplicity: rows of neat quarter notes
march along the sheet music in large print, like rhythmic clapping
exercises for senior citizens. The melodies are also simple. Short,
undemanding phrases repeat across the page at a slow tempo.

But then, right in the middle of a simple musical phrase, the
notes launch into the violin's stratosphere—sometimes called the

nose-picking section since the violinist's fingers are so close to the face—where the highest pitches are produced. Playing super-high notes at a slow tempo is a musical tightrope walk. The higher up the violin one goes, the closer together the fingers must be to hit the right note, and the more obvious it is if the fingers are off by even a fraction of a millimeter. Unlike the lower regions of the instrument, where the fingers can vibrato or sway to create a frequency that mathematically averages into the right pitch, the highest notes on a violin are too close together to allow for much, if any, movement. A wayward speck of cuticle crust on a violinist's finger can cause a high note to become painful to hear—audience members will instinctively reach for their ears.

You puzzle over these passages, your fingers tapping calculations on the fingerboard. Despite your years of lessons, you never fully mastered the treacherous nose-picking section. You are not even fluent in reading the highest notes, a deficit that forces you to keep playing scales while you practice so that you can climb, as if on a musical safety ladder, to the correct top note.

Panicked by the sheet music, you lie down on your dorm room bed, your violin resting on your stomach. You close your eyes and focus on listening to one of The Composer's CDs from start to finish. Simple string melodies sweep into quick climaxes, buttressed by the high wail of an Irish-sounding flute. It is like listening to a synthetic sea—the sound of one wave blending into the next—languid, insistent, and faintly menacing.

Like movie soundtracks, The Composer's albums feature one or two distinct melodies that have been slightly altered or rearranged on each track to produce a new "song." The songs are short and don't appear to be organized in any particular order, any particular chronology. The feeling you get from listening to them can only be described as watching yourself from a distance, as if you were a character in someone else's implausibly dramatic movie.

West Virginia

1985

You ask your parents for a violin for your fifth birthday. When no violin arrives, you ask for a violin for Christmas. Then again for your sixth birthday. Seventh. Eighth. There are no violin teachers in your region of West Virginia, your parents explain. Not even Santa can fix this problem.

You beg your parents to rent *Sarah and the Squirrel* again from the town's dusty video rental shop, but they refuse. Eventually the VHS disappears from the rental's shelves. But the music from *Sarah and the Squirrel* remains in your head. You think of this music as "Brahms" for nearly a decade, until one day, at thirteen years old, you hear a recording of Vivaldi's "Winter" and the synapses of musical memory in your brain explode into applause. Another decade later, in your twenties, you find a copy of *Sarah and the Squirrel* on eBay and confirm that the music is, indeed, Vivaldi's "Winter." But before these discoveries, you are vigilant against forgetting this music. You play the music inside of your head each night in bed before falling asleep, your eyes tracing the comet-shaped plaster crevices on your bedroom ceiling. You play the music each night to remember it, because you *must* remember it. The music makes you feel something that is not quite sadness, but not happiness either. These particular notes that you heard only once make you feel something akin to seriousness. *What is this seriousness?* you wonder. Eventually you realize: The seriousness of the *Sarah* music is the same as the seriousness of the adult world. You have found the key—serious music—that will unlock the secrets of being a grown-up.

Your desire to be grown up is inextricably linked with your desire to do the one thing that is most revered by the adults around you: work. Work is in the Appalachian air you breathe, in the coal smoke of the nearby Mount Storm Power Station, which channels electricity to much of the East Coast, each unit of coal someone's work, someone's dinner, someone's television running all night on low volume until it's morning and time to return to work. At school you have "workbooks" and "worksheets" and you complete yours as fast as you can, so that you can do more work. You aim to get more work done than any other kid, for this will surely result in you being more loved than any other kid. Minutes after getting off the school bus you set to strong-arming your little brother into "playing school," a game in which you assign him "homework" and yell at him when he refuses to do it. But the game you most want to play is music, a serious game that even serious adults "play."

If you could play the music from *Sarah and the Squirrel*, you would unlock all adult mysteries. You sense secrets everywhere, perhaps because many of your elementary school friends are going through their own personal versions of *Sarah and the Squirrel*—lives full of hunger and cold and abuse—though whatever Dickensian nightmare they inhabit survives in your memory only as hazy images: the boy who smells like garbage and scratches his tiny, scab-covered body until he bleeds all over his desk. The pale girl who smells like cigarettes and steals your favorite purple pencil. The boy who wears the same torn-to-hell red sweatsuit every day and screams "JACK-ASS!" at the gym teacher while kicking the brick school wall with his disintegrating sneaker. The cagey look that makes some of the quieter boys look like frightened rabbits. The names of the kids in your class that invoke mountain fate, branded at birth, an inescapable geographical destiny: Stony, Dusty, Misty.

As your young ears strain to hear the world's secrets through a few remembered notes, your parents inhabit a world with too few secrets. Your social worker mom drives up the icy switchbacks of mountainsides to deliver WIC stamps and vaccinations to people living in one-room shacks. She arrives at one home with the intention of teaching a mother how to play with her toddler with toys on the floor, only to discover that the house has no floor—just five inches of tramped-down soot from the wood stove. On another visit, she notices a baby sleeping in a bureau drawer, a few inches away from a coiled copperhead.

Your dad, a family practice doctor running a clinic for the rural poor, also makes house calls. He carries an actual old-fashioned black doctor's bag full of tongue depressors and bandage wrap. He treats patients suffering the botched results of mountain-home remedies: abscesses turned gangrenous after being wrapped in deerskin poultices, the bloody infected sockets where rotten teeth once festered before being partially pried out with a farm tool. Then one day a flood sweeps through the gorge and washes your dad's clinic away. He takes out a large loan, rebuilds the clinic, and works punishing hours, sometimes taking patient payments in jam, beans, and on one occasion a five-gallon bucket of peas—your mom hunches to shell them while nine-months pregnant with your brother.

One January evening a patient drives up to your house and offers payment in the currency of sweet summer corn, frozen on the cob. Your dad, making the most of the occasion, moves the family supper table to the back porch and, even though it is dark and snowy outside with wind shrieking down the mountainsides, everyone munches salted corncobs while wearing winter coats. The idea is to pretend it's July.

And maybe this is why, as you get older, you increasingly feel that there is something secret and menacing around you: Your parents are working so hard ("You have to work hard" is one of their favorite expressions) to alchemize mountain snow into tropical sunshine, to munch merrily on corncobs, as if your mom isn't handing out pre-scriptions for food all day; as if your dad hasn't just staged a mass rabies inoculation (someone brought a pet raccoon into a trailer park full of kids); as if your teenage babysitter hasn't attempted suicide by overdosing on pills while she was supposed to be watching you (she was still better than West Virginia day care, your mom points out, years later). You know the sinister music in your head is important because it speaks of something true about your world, something that the adults are attempting to hide from you (*It's summertime! Don't forget your coat!*). No doubt they are doing this to protect you, a child, from the harshness of the Appalachian poverty and despair that surrounds you. What they don't realize is that their very effort to conceal this harshness is what tips you off to its existence.

The taste of parsley is one of your earliest memories; your grand-mother plucking it from a patch that grows a few feet away from your grandfather's yard-pile of old broken lightbulbs. This is just the sort of inconsistency—a plentiful, parsley-flavored middle-class life among the broken ruins of coal-fired poverty—that you begin to notice as a kid.

Picking around the carcass of a wrecked car on a mountainside ravine near your grandparents' house—in an Appalachian paper mill town where the air has a permanent sulfuric stink—you find a jam jar with an unmarred red gingham label still displaying ripened red strawberries. But the jar is full of dirt. You wonder how the dirt got in there, since the lid of the jar is still sealed tight. You can recognize hypocrisy in a dirt-filled jam jar, taste it in parsley that grows in a trash garden, smell it in the kerosene heat, the cigarette smoke, the paper mill stink, the booze-crazed eyes, the chicken-guts smell that clings to the kids whose parents work at the plant. ("Your kids goin' to Chicken Plant University?" another doctor asks your dad. "I hear the tuition is *cheep cheep*!" A not-joking joke in a town where even some of the most well-off kids drop out of high school to work at the plant. One girl your age, who lives a few miles up the road from your grandparents' house, will witness "chicken-stomping" at this very plant, a practice that disgusts her so much she decides to quit her job there and join the army, figuring that the army can't be any worse than chicken-stomping. Her name is Lynndie England.)

You don't know what to do with the jam jar, the chicken stink, the sinister mountain fog that is everywhere, but the adults pretend to ignore when you are in the room. It seems the only thing you can do is listen for it. You hear it in the four measures of Vivaldi's "Winter" that you can still remember from *Sarah and the Squirrel*, and once you make the connection between the music and the mountain fog you play the notes over and over again inside your head.

You paw up the trash-strewn ravine. The sky is low and gray, the color of the cinder blocks the men in your town manufacture from ash and dust. The dirt-filled strawberry jam jar is in your denim coat pocket. Vivaldi is in your head. The music you hear is like the blaze-orange clothing the men wear on the mountainsides while deer hunting in autumn. The music is like a bulletproof vest, a coiled copperhead, a rabies shot. The music is both a warning and a talisman. The music tells you things: *You're not imagining this. Better children than you die in the snow for no reason.*

The music says: *What's hidden beneath this picture of strawberry jam?*

The music says: *This isn't a Disney movie. Death doesn't just take the wicked villain. Look at that dirt in the jam jar. It will take you. It will take everyone, and everyone, and everyone.*

The music says: *What you feel is real. Follow me. Run.*

New York City
2002

Y ou wait for Yevgeny, the Russian violinist, at the northwest corner of 115th and Broadway. You have just gotten off an eight-hour shift as a receptionist for a ritzy uptown spa and are still wearing the mandatory uniform—a white shirt, khakis, and red sneakers. You sip on your dinner: a strawberry milkshake. You recently dyed your black hair to a shade of smoldering maroon, and with your red hair, your red shoes, your mini-backpack, and your pink milkshake, it occurs to you that you look more like a preteen on her way to a babysitting gig than a twenty-one-year-old soon-to-be professional violinist. You ditch the milkshake.

A white sedan pulls up to the corner and a tall, thin man steps out. Without introducing himself, he points at your small book bag and asks, "That's all you're bringing?"

Having pictured him as the rotund, jolly, bearded father from *Fiddler on the Roof*, you are surprised that the real Yevgeny is so young—no more than twenty-five years old. He has white-blond hair, pale skin, and a facial expression that suggests resigned gloom.

You take your place in the passenger seat and he throws a Satellite Radio instruction manual in your lap.

"Pick some music," he says as he pulls away from the curb.

You search for a classical station, thinking that when it comes to long car rides to New Hampshire with gloomy Russian violinists, it's best to play it safe with the music. As a Berlioz symphony reaches its climax, the frantic entanglements of the Bronx yield to the tunnels of foliage that line Interstate 95 in southern Connecticut. Yevgeny stares at the road ahead of him in a determined silence that makes you feel awkward, as if you have both been forced on a blind date. You make a few attempts to discuss the classical music on the radio, but Yevgeny doesn't respond. You stare out the window.

An hour or so into the trip, you ask him what music he likes to listen to, other than classical.

"Mostly techno," he says.

"Oh," you say, and turn the station from "Symphony Hall" to "Electric Area," transforming the car from an eighteenth-century Austrian concert hall into a Brooklyn rave circa 1997.

"So what is this gig like?" you ask, trying to sound like a professional musician who uses the word "gig" casually.

Yevgeny doesn't respond to your question for a long time, as if pondering the futility of human speech.

"What do you want to know?" he finally asks.

"Um . . . well, I listened to the music on the CDs . . ."

"And?"

"It's nice . . ."

"You like it?" he demands.

"Well, I mean, to be honest, I'd never heard of The Composer before I was hired." You hope this information won't be used against you.

Yevgeny hunches over the steering wheel and glares at the road.

"So, who is he?" you ask timidly. "Who is The Composer?"

"He writes the music," Yevgeny says.

"I know, but who *is* he?" you insist. "I mean, like, have you met him?"

"Yes."

"What's he like?"

"I don't know. He's weird."

"Have you worked for him a long time?"

"A few years."

"Where did you study violin?"

"Moscow Conservatory."

"Wow," you say. "That's the best . . ."

"Listen, by tomorrow, you'll want to quit," Yevgeny says. He looks at you, and you realize he is actually concerned. "Before this job I worked at a butcher's shop. I didn't speak much English. I almost sliced off my fingers . . ." He trails off for a moment.

"The only reason anyone stays in this job," he continues, "is because they're desperate. I doubt that you're desperate."

You want to respond that you are, in fact, plenty desperate; that for the past three years you have been selling everything from long-distance telephone scams to massage oils to your own eggs, which fetch you tens of thousands of dollars on the Upper East Side egg donation market—all to pay for your college tuition. But you don't say anything about this. Not yet. Instead, you decide to tell Yevgeny the truth about your musical skills.

"I should tell you something," you say carefully. "I'm not a real violinist."

Yevgeny doesn't respond. The setting sun reflects off his white-blond hair, giving him the look of a regal bird.

"What I mean is," you say, backpedaling, "I was pretty good in high school but my high school was in the middle of nowhere—like Appalachia? Do you know where it is? Yes? Okay . . . and I've barely taken lessons in college and I'd be lucky to make it into the back row of a college orchestra and I haven't trained at Julliard or Moscow Conservatory and, honestly, I don't even know why Becca hired me, it must have been a mistake, but I feel so lucky to even be here, so you don't need to worry about me quitting because *I'm* the one who should be worried because I mean *you're* a real professional . . ."

Yevgeny is laughing. His laugh is distinctly Russian, more of a sly chuckle than a raucous guffaw, raucous guffaws having been outlawed during Soviet times. Still, making Yevgeny laugh feels like a great accomplishment, even if you have no idea what is so funny.

"Don't worry," he says. "You're going to do fine. Everything will make sense tomorrow, you'll see. Don't worry about it anymore tonight. Are you hungry?"

"Are you?"

He pulls into a Burger King, adding that he never allows stops on these road trips because he can't stand most of the other Ensemble musicians. You beam at this circuitous compliment, at the idea that Yevgeny likes you, or at least finds you less annoying than other people. You order the kid's meal and it comes with a toy—scratch-and-sniff stickers that look and smell like feet, boogers, and armpits. As you eat, Yevgeny scratches and sniffs each sticker, first with caution, then with increasing glee.

"It *does* smell like a fute!" he exclaims, scratching and sniffing the foot sticker over and over. He pronounces "foot" as "fute." "Try it! Try it! It smells like a fute—a real fute!"

"I take it there are no foot stickers that come with your cheeseburgers in Moscow?"

"No," he says, taking another deep sniff. "Only America has fake fute smell. If you want to smell fute in Moscow, you have to smell a real fute."

Needmore, West Virginia
1989

You don't remember if the car died suddenly, or if the engine slowly dwindled to silence. You don't remember if there was smoke from a blown transmission or if it was an electrical failure. All you remember is your dad carrying your violin in one hand, holding your hand in the other, as you abandoned the car in an isolated holler called Needmore ("Needmore!" you'd shout as you drove through on better days. "You Need-more people!"). Hand in hand, the two of you begin to walk. The nearest gas station (and pay phone) is over the next mountain, a 2,000-foot vertical climb and descent. It is late afternoon in early spring; the holler is dark and cold. But there you are: a father, his eight-year-old daughter, her pint-size violin, and a 2,000-foot mountain. An Appalachian tableau of a family on its way to the upper-middle class.

When your dad was ten years old his own father died suddenly, plunging his once prosperous Washington, D.C., family into poverty. Perhaps because he lost his own father so early, your dad values time with you and your brothers above all things. The idea of driving together to violin lessons—hours of uninterrupted time in the car—appeals to him. Your mom, on the other hand, is more practical. Her large energetic Italian immigrant family worked their way toward the American Dream in the West Virginia mills and mines. You imagine the conversations your parents must have had about your request, your dad saying *Violin lessons? Why not!*, your mom listing all the sensible reasons for why not (four to six hours of driving over the mountains each week, for starters).

But on your eighth birthday, there it is: a three-quarter-size violin, the thing you have most wanted, the shield against mountain fog, the talisman against fake, corncob-colored sunshine. And it comes with another, even more generous present: weekly violin lessons in Virginia. In the days before your first lesson you open the hard black case and run your fingers over the shiny amber wood and bleached white horsehair. You slide one of your fingers underneath the strings and pluck them while thinking the words *fragile* and *delicate*, words that you like because they sound like what they mean. You put your nostrils over the instrument's f-holes and inhale the varnishy scent. You glide the amber-colored cube of unmarred pinesap rosin out of its pink box and smell it, too. You push the palms of your hands against the plush blue lining of the case, snap and unsnap the case's shiny silver lock. You take the violin out of its case and cradle it with more care than when you hold your two-month-old baby brother.

The next Tuesday, after a two-hour drive to Virginia with your dad, you arrive at a sun-filled house, where a room with hardwood floors and enormous windows serves as a music studio. The first thing you tell your teacher, who is young and pretty with long, curly hair, is that you want to learn how to play a song you heard once, four years ago, when you were four. In a squirrel cartoon.

She opens your violin case and takes out the instrument with startling quickness.

You persist about the song. She must know it. After all, it is violin music and she is a violin teacher.

"Do you know the *name* of the song?" she asks while tightening your bow.

You do not. But you can sing it for her. Except, it's impossible to sing a song composed for a twenty-piece Baroque ensemble playing five parts plus harpsichord. But you try anyway. Now, years of musical training later, you can explain in technical terms what you did: You sang four equal beats of one pitch, lowered your pitch by a perfect fifth for another four beats, raised your pitch by a diminished fourth for four beats, and then lowered it again by a perfect fifth for the last four beats. Those are the technical specifications of the four measures of the main theme from the first movement of Vivaldi's "Winter." But the technical language feels empty. It does not explain why it was so important to you, at eight years old, to know this music better. It does not explain why these four measures of music had come to represent your most important thoughts about yourself and the wild, unknowable world around you.

"I don't know it," your teacher says with a tone of finality, and she shows you how to rosin your bow.

"Maybe it is Brahms," you suggest.

"Maybe," she says.

"It's music about Anne Frank," you insist.

This gets her attention. She looks at you and then your dad. Your dad starts to explain, stops, and shrugs.

"Let's start with 'Twinkle, Twinkle,'" she says.

As she introduces the rhythmic variations on "Twinkle, Twinkle, Little Star"—the standard beginning lesson in the Suzuki method—your mood plummets. She demonstrates the four variations by using silly mnemonic devices that mimic the four basic rhythms: *Mississippi Hotdog*, *Peanuts and Popcorn*, *Run Pony Run Pony*, and *Mississippi Alabama*.

Your dad, who is observing in the corner, loves this idea.

"West Virginia Coleslaw, West Virginia Coleslaw," he starts singing.

"Ha! That's right!" your teacher smiles at him. "You could use that instead of Mississippi Hotdog."

"Mississippi Indigestion, Mississippi Indigestion!" he sings, getting carried away.

You fume inside. You have not spent years begging for a violin to waste time fooling around with kid stuff like hotdogs and ponies. You want to understand the seriousness of life and death, the creeping fog.

In the weeks afterward, you practice "helicoptering" your bow onto the strings. The idea is not to crash, but to land gently, like a butterfly. You are skeptical of this idea. You might be a little girl, the smallest little girl in your second-grade class, but you are no butterfly. You are loud and chatty and move around too much and bang into things. Your parents and teachers are always telling you to "settle down." Every day you practice helicoptering your bow and every day you become more aware that your violin is going to demand things from you that have never been demanded, a level of focus and precision that you are not sure you can give. But after a few weeks of work so hard that your face sweats as you helicopter over and over again, your bow lands on the strings as silent as a moth. The first lesson in making music, it turns out, is making silence—the blank canvas, the empty room, the white page. A void that must be made before it can be filled.

The guiding philosophy of the Suzuki method is that children should learn music as if it were a language, and that they should begin lessons as early as possible, ideally at the age of two and no later than five. Research by Oliver Sacks and others has confirmed this claim. After a certain age—somewhere between eight and twelve years old—the window for learning a spoken or musical language with native-level proficiency slams shut. As an eight-year-old scratching out your first notes of "Twinkle, Twinkle," you are the musical equivalent of an eight-year-old who has never spoken a word: already years behind.

Because you had begged your parents to take lessons, and not the other way around, you are more motivated to learn than other students. (You will discover that most kids who take violin lessons say that their parents "make" them do it, an idea you find puzzling.) Even so, you are overwhelmed with the daily realization of just how difficult learning to play the instrument will be. It takes months before you can play a recognizable tune, and the endless scratching and screeching offers no positive reinforcement, just boredom and a sense of futility, not to mention a painful throbbing in the soft neck tissue under your chin and sore fingertips that flake like paper and burn like chapped lips.

But the weekly journeys to violin lessons are not just about you—they involve your entire family, and everyone is becoming exhausted. You live in a town that is surrounded by mountains, a region of dramatic, steep cliffs and plateaus that form the Eastern Continental Divide in Appalachia. Getting to your violin lessons in Virginia requires driving over a half-dozen wheel-spinning, stomach-churning, ear-popping mountains on the West Virginia state highway system—a series of potholed secondary roads with no passing lanes. Eighteen-wheelers filled with coal or live chickens gasp up the mountains and zoom down, sometimes losing control of their brakes. The entire trip, including your thirty-minute violin lesson, takes anywhere between five to eight hours, and that's if there isn't a freak mountain blizzard.

Every Tuesday at 1:30 p.m. you leave your second-grade class-room two hours early and walk outside to the mountain-shadowed parking lot. On the few Tuesdays when your dad isn't working, he waits there in his Nissan. You head through the first mountain gorge and then he stops at a gas station for snacks—Fritos and Coke for him, Oreos and strawberry milk for you. After your lesson, he takes you to eat fried noodles with duck sauce and wonton soup at a Chinese restaurant in a college town of 22,000 residents. It might as well be Hong Kong for how cosmopolitan it seems to you, a girl from an isolated town of 2,000 people and no McDonalds, let alone a Chinese restaurant. On the way back home, your dad plays his new cassette tape of *Les Misérables*, despite the fact that it is full of curse words and prostitutes. He explains the French Revolution to you as though you can understand it, and you feel like you *do* understand it, that people who are cold and hungry might get so angry that they'd burst out singing in forceful British accents. You ask him to play and replay Cosette's lament, which evokes the general idea of the mountain fog, though not as well as Vivaldi's music. Still, the *Les Misérables* tape becomes another way in which you equate childhood sadness with music, perhaps because by equating despair with music, you don't have to equate it with the faces of your second-grade classmates, who are rowdier, meaner, stinkier, and more humanly complex than the silvery-voiced, one-dimensional, fictional orphan Cosette.

Trips to violin lessons with your dad allow you to pretend, for at least a few hours, that you are not an eight-year-old girl wearing a pink "Almost Heaven: West Virginia" t-shirt with a rainbow and unicorn on it, but are instead a serious adult person with serious adult person things to say. His attention to you and only you makes you feel important, special, loved, and, most of all, grown up. But

more often, violin-lesson duty falls to your mom, who is on mater-
nity leave from her job. With your dad at work, she retrieves one
brother out of kindergarten and buckles the other brother into an
infant car seat. With the four of you loaded into a Dodge minivan,
there is no pretending that you are anything but what you are—a
kid whose whole family is sacrificing a lot to give her something
she wants. The baby wails in pain from the ear-popping altitude
change every time you ascend or descend a mountain. Your mom
comforts him while navigating treacherous mountain curves and
icy patches—coal trucks on one side of the road, sheer cliffs on the
other. After your lesson she straps everyone back into the minivan
and drives through a KFC window for baked chicken, biscuits, and
plain milk. Then the long drive back, this time in the dark. While
driving, your mom tests you on your multiplication tables and your
kindergartener brother on his ABCs. She instructs you on how to
feed the baby and pulls over to wipe the vomit off your shirt when
someone gets carsick. When she wants everyone to shut up—what
she calls "quiet time"—she pops in one of the two cassette tapes that
reside in the minivan: *Wee Sing Silly Songs* ("There's a hole in the
bucket, dear Liza dear Liza!") and a Disney soundtrack compilation
("Look for the bare necessities—old Mother Nature's recipes!").
Two to four hours later, you climb out of the minivan exhausted and
nauseated, your face plastered with biscuit crumbs, chicken grease,
and baby spit, your ears ringing with "Bibbidi-Bobbidi-Boo."

If someone had asked you at eight years old what the point of
these weekly trips were, you would have given the simple answer:
The point of these journeys was the violin lesson, even though
sometimes you never made it to the actual violin lesson. (After your
dad's car breaks down in the chilly holler of Needmore, the two of
you walk hand in hand along the roadside, toward the two thousand-

foot mountain. Your dad sticks out his thumb to passing cars and four West Virginia gals in a pickup truck stop in front of you. Your dad climbs into the open truck bed while you sit inside the cabin on one gal's lap. The women offer you a wine cooler, to which you reply with a polite "No, thank you," which makes them laugh. As the truck hauls ass up the mountain, you swivel your body around, checking to make sure your dad hasn't been flung over the side of a cliff. He sees the expression on your face and waves at you, smiles, gives you the thumbs-up.) But years later, as you find yourself traveling tens of thousands of miles across America as a professional violinist for the The Composer's Ensemble, it strikes you that in addition to the violin lessons themselves, you received weekly lessons about being on the road. How far you have to go and how much it takes out of you (and the people around you) just to get to a place where it's possible to learn something.

First Gig
New Hampshire, 2002

After an eight-hour drive from New York City and a night in a hotel, Yevgeny pulls the car up to a grassy yard with tents in Wolfeboro, a town near Lake Winnipesaukee. The scent of grease-fried sugar wafts out from a funnel cake vendor. Children line up at a face-painting station. The sights and smells remind you of something familiar, though you have never before associated it with the world of classical music: the county fair.

But it isn't exactly a county fair—it is much too small. Becca had called it an "art fair" and you had pictured something fancier, something like Tanglewood—more "art" than "craft." But this gathering is most certainly about the crafts: fabric purses, handmade candles and soaps, wooden wind chimes. Even though the fair has not yet officially begun, dozens of middle-aged women wearing bright sun visors and Capri pants cluster around the vendors' tables.

Yevgeny lugs a canopy tent to a designated spot in the maze of tents and sets it up. He runs back to the car to get the amplifier, microphone stands, and speakers. His eyes are puffy with fatigue, his skin a yellowish-gray, his pale hair slicked to a level of comic Russian severity. He wears a long-sleeve black shirt with black dress pants and black shoes. What he looks like is a Hollywood parody of a KGB agent, complete with a carefully guarded black case, which one might mistake for a sniper's rifle rather than a violin. The other craft fair vendors—middle-aged Americans wearing t-shirts and shorts—stare at Yevgeny in terror.

You begin to unpack the boxes of CDs, but you pause when you come across a box full of VHS tapes. Unlike the CDs, which feature glossy nature photographs on their covers, the VHS tape cover has a crudely drawn cartoon of a ship. It is titled *The Composer: The Pirate*.

The pirate?

You want to ask whether The Composer is, in fact, a pirate, but Yevgeny is busy attaching a Sony Discman to the amplifier. He takes what appears to be a blank CD and puts it in the Discman. "We don't play all the songs," he tells you. "This CD is just the 'greatest hits.'"

"So how will I tell the customers which song is on which CD?" you ask. "I still can't tell all of the songs apart."

"It won't matter," Yevgeny says. He gestures at the crowds of women who are clustering around the sales table and whispers, "They won't know the difference either."

You are still pondering this when Debbie, the flute player, arrives, having driven to Wolfeboro from her nearby home. She appears to be in her twenties and has red hair, an ample bosom, and a British accent. She's wearing pink pants, pink athletic shoes, and a black t-shirt—concert attire that clashes with Yevgeny's all-black KGB outfit. She gives you a wary once-over and then turns to Yevgeny.

"Have I been fired yet?" she asks him.

"No, you're not that lucky," Yevgeny replies. "Are you ready?"

Debbie nods and takes a plastic pennywhistle out of her purse. Yevgeny pushes the Play button on the Sony Discman.

The small hairs on your face and arms are dancing—a chilling, vibrating sway. You stare into the mouths of the speakers, which are only a few feet away and seem to be emitting a stiff breeze. It takes you a moment to realize that the wind you feel on your face is actually sound. Your rib cage vibrates; sound waves buzz and bounce around cavities that must be your lungs. For a moment, you lose your breath.

It is loud. Rock concert loud.

You stare at Yevgeny and Debbie. Debbie is blowing through a pennywhistle—a Celtic flute similar to the plastic recorders kids play in elementary school. Yevgeny is bowing the strings of his violin. But it doesn't seem possible for such a loud sound to be coming out of these two instruments, especially not a violin. Then again, you have never played with an amplifier and background music before. Maybe that is what makes the sound so . . . so . . . perfect.

For that is what it is: Sound that is unbelievably polished, especially for the low-quality acoustics of an outdoor setting. *They sound damn good for two people playing in an open-air tent*, you think, staring at them with your mouth agape, which causes your teeth and gums to vibrate.

Yevgeny glares back at you and makes a jutting motion with his chin. You realize he is motioning for you to pay attention to the customers. You spin around to find that there is a crowd of almost fifty people in front of you. Where did they all come from? How did they get here so fast? Their hands are all over the CDs, obliterating the neat stacks you made minutes before, their eyes squinting at the pricing chart: One CD for $12, two for $22, all the way up to ten for $80. And then, for the first time, you hear the question that you will hear, word for word, thousands of times over the next four years:

"What's he playing now?"

You jump into action. "This one!" you yell over the din of the speakers, shoving copies of *Morning Meadow* into everyone's hands. While the customers examine the CDs, scrutinizing the meadow cover art as if it might yield clues about the music, Yevgeny and Debbie launch into another song, from another album. Debbie emits a piercing melody on the pennywhistle that sounds very familiar, though you can't place it. "What's he playing *now*?" the customers demand. Their numbers are multiplying. You push copies of *Oceans of April* into as many palms as you can, the plastic wrappings on the CDs pulsing with sound vibrations underneath your fingertips.

And then comes the money. It comes at you from all directions. From loud, sun-burnt ladies and their shy, baseball-capped husbands:

I'll take this one and this one. Oh! And this one!

What's he playing now?

This one?

Hey, Jean! This is what he's playing now!

Oh my God! It's so relaxing! It's beautiful!

Is that The Composer?

"No," you shout. "That is Yevgeny."

Well, who is The Composer?

I'll take five CDs over here!

"He's . . . um . . . a composer. He writes the music."

He's not here?

"No. But here's a picture of him," you shout, pointing at The Composer's photo on the cover of *The Composer: Live from New York.* You stare at this photo for a moment. It was taken at Alice Tully Hall at Lincoln Center. The Composer looks young and strikingly handsome. He is thin and square-jawed with a healthy mop of brunette hair that looks precisely the way a tortured composer's mop of brunette hair should. He is wearing a blue-trimmed tuxedo and his conductor's baton is frozen in the middle of a dramatic upbeat. *If Hollywood made a movie about a serious conductor,* you think, *they would cast someone who looks exactly like The Composer.*

But who *is* The Composer?

The customers keep asking, "What is *he* playing?" You are puzzled by their refusal to acknowledge Debbie, but you soon realize that most of the customers still think Yevgeny is The Composer.

Some customers are already familiar with The Composer's music. "I already have this CD and this CD," these veteran customers say. "So I need to get this one and this one."

And some customers have even met The Composer in the flesh.

"I remember when The Composer played at Maine Mall," one man says. "How is he?"

"Oh, fine," you reply, unsure if it is okay to admit you've never met the guy. "He's doing just great."

The more you attempt to answer inquiries about The Composer's character and whereabouts, the more you become intrigued by the mystery of him, a man making thousands of dollars in CD sales without showing up to his own concert. You picture The Composer wearing his conductor's tuxedo while reclining on a beach chair and sipping a daiquiri. You picture The Composer trekking through the Amazon, swatting at mosquitoes with his conductor's baton. You picture The Composer marching through Europe, piping on a pennywhistle, a dancing crowd of street urchins following behind him.

"Miss! Miss! What's he playing now?"

You shove the album *Oceans of April* into their hands.

"It sounds like *Titanic*!" a customer yells.

The other customers agree. "It does—it's *Titanic*! He's playing *Titanic*!"

You nod warily, unsure whether they think this is a good or bad thing, although it is, without a doubt, a very true thing. You hadn't realized it until now, but the song that Yevgeny and Debbie are playing is sharply similar to Céline Dion's famous ballad "My Heart Will Go On." But it's been almost five years since the movie was released. Do these people really want to buy a knockoff of an old movie soundtrack?

I love Titanic! the customers shriek.

You collect handfuls and handfuls of cash. If you sell over $5,000 worth of CDs, you and the musicians will each receive a $50 bonus. You can already tell that you are going to top $5,000 in sales, which, considering the bargain prices and the backyard-like location of the concert, is a lot of CDs.

After several more customers mention *Titanic*, you begin to realize that most of The Composer's compositions sound very *Titanic*-esque. And you notice that the more the songs sound like *Titanic*, the more the customers want to buy them.

God Bless America Tour 2004

Atlanta

B ecause we play along with a CD, our concerts never change, have no chance of spontaneity or deviation from the norm. Every night The Composer presses Play and we go along, like musical machines. Patrick mans the film projectors and watches us from the back of the auditorium. His arms are folded across his chest, the corners of his blue eyes moist with tears, his mustache quivering.

The concerts begin with the song "Sea Flower." The keyboard and violins open the piece, but like second-tier ballerinas we are dancing on the side of the stage, setting the scene for the real star. By the fifth measure, as is the case with all The Composer's songs, the pennywhistle—the prima ballerina—steals the show. The pennywhistle's first notes are in the lower register of the instrument, but then the tune soars upward, higher and higher to the utmost rafters of the human ear. On the giant projector screens an eagle flies high in the sky, then swoops downward toward the Grand Canyon.

The impact on the audience is a sort of emotional hostage-taking: YOU WILL FEEL SOMETHING VERY POWERFUL RIGHT NOW, the eagle sings in the voice of a pennywhistle. YOU WILL SWELL WITH VAGUE BUT IMPORTANT-FEELING EMOTIONS FOR NO DISCERNABLE REASON. Then, the violins return for a few sighing measures, as if to say, let's be reasonable. Can't we just have a nice, calm, sensible song? NO, the pennywhistle-voiced eagle responds. I DEMAND ALL OF YOUR EMOTIONS. GIMMEE! GIMMEE! So the violins go along with it, climbing higher and higher into their nose-picking regions. The high-definition nature footage sweeps the audience over the Maine coast, over bucolic dunes and quaint lighthouses until—lo, the Atlantic! Spread out like time immortal! You, the audience member, are flying! You are the eagle!

An Important Reality

New Hampshire, 2002

During the course of your first day as an employee of The Composer's Ensemble, a subtle but crucial reality begins to dawn on you: The audience members at the craft fair can hear very little of the sound that Yevgeny and Debbie are producing with their instruments. While Debbie's pennywhistle is shrill enough to be heard for the highest notes, Yevgeny's violin is almost inaudible against the blast of the background track.

This realization comes in stages. It is obvious from the start that the speakers are very loud, far louder than the loudest sound that can be produced by a violin. You scrutinize Yevgeny's fingers. Yes, he *is* actually playing. There isn't a way to "half-play" or "fake-play" a violin or flute, especially after years of learning how to play for real. They *are* playing, but standing only a few feet away, you aren't hearing them. Whatever sounds they are making are being drowned in a shiny sea of CD-produced music. The microphones in front of them are turned to the lowest volume (later, when you begin playing at the gigs, the microphone in front of you will often be dead). What you are hearing, instead, is a flawless, audio-mixed studio recording of other musicians playing the same music. This is why it sounds so good. This is why the customers are so enraptured.

When the human ear hears the sound of a violin, and the human eye sees a black-clad Russian violinist playing, the human brain does not stop to question whether these two phenomena are related. The "concert" you are witnessing, you begin to realize, is an optical illusion. A very, very good one.

In between customers, you steal sly looks at Yevgeny. His playing form is effortless. If you angle your ear behind the giant speaker, you can sometimes manage to hear a few notes he is producing; they are pitched to perfection with a beautiful, distinct tone that could only be produced by this particular human being with this particular violin. After a few hours, he begins to play with his eyes closed. Debbie stares into space with a bored expression. Good performing violinists often appear to produce sound with their whole bodies, every tendon and nerve on high alert. But Yevgeny and Debbie look like two middle school students in the back row of an orchestra they have been forced to join. They look lazy. Listless. Bored.

As the day wears on, you realize why Yevgeny and Debbie perform in such a lackadaisical state. It isn't laziness; it's conservation of energy. Most orchestral performances include breaks: within the music itself, between the songs, at intermission. And most concerts last no more than an hour or two, including those breaks. But Yevgeny and Debbie have been performing nonstop in two-hour sets for eight hours, with only a few minutes' pause between sets and a thirty-minute break for lunch. The craft fair concert, you now realize, is more of an athletic challenge than a musical one, akin to dribbling a basketball for eight hours—easy at first, but difficult after an hour or so. With the temperature in the tent in the high eighties, you wonder how Yevgeny, dressed from head to foot in black, is still standing.

But from where you stand at the CD seller's table, The Composer's music drifts on the breeze, pulsing the small hairs on the back of your neck. You feel a powerful surge of exhilarating contentment. You are young and free and you have the world's best job. Anything can happen. You are the luckiest girl in the world!

And suddenly, you have a disconcerting thought: The Composer's music is artificially enhancing your emotions—the way a film soundtrack makes a banal conversation between lovers seem epic. Yevgeny and Debbie are playing a piece called "Ocean's Cliff." It begins with soft, rolling piano chords—the acoustic of water—and a pennywhistle solo that sounds like a sea spirit beckoning from the deep. And then the violin joins in with dramatic octaves, like waves. You *are* happy, it *is* your first day of work as a professional musician, and the New England summer day is all lush sunshine, soft grass, warm breeze. But like a psychedelic drug, the music is augmenting the colors around you, amplifying your happiness until the moment feels more significant than other moments of happiness, as if this is *the* most important moment of happiness in your life. You realize that you have just experienced your first Composer-induced trance, a flying-at-the-bow-of-a-ship-and-Leo-is-kissing-you moment.

Later, after an afternoon rush of customers has dispersed, Yevgeny asks if you would like to try playing a few songs on his violin.

"Yes!" you shout, brushing funnel cake crumbs off your hands and leaping to take his violin from him.

"Start with 'Autumn Radiance,'" Yevgeny says. "It's the easiest one."

"No problem," you say, shaking out your shoulders like a gymnast about to jump onto the balance beam.

You lift Yevgeny's violin to your chin, angling it toward the microphone. Yevgeny pushes the Play button on the Sony Discman. You look at your sheet music, but you can't find your place. If you don't know where the beat is, you have no hope of counting your way into the place where you are supposed to begin playing. In an orchestra, the conductor inhales a gulp of air right before the first downbeat of his baton. The orchestra breathes with him and that's how everyone starts at the same time, breathing together, like one organism with forty sets of lungs. But with no conductor and no discernable downbeats, you are still holding your breath.

Yevgeny stops the CD. He looks annoyed.

"You're waiting too long," he says.

"Right," you answer, embarrassed.

He presses Play again.

This time you start at the right place, but after just a few notes you lose your way again. From behind the speakers, the CD is difficult to hear. You are in a musical vortex, thrashing out random bow strokes this way and that, hurling wrong notes in every direction. Any moment now Yevgeny will call off the whole attempt and grab his violin from your unworthy fingers.

Instead, he shrugs and turns his attention toward a crowd of new customers. After three minutes that feel like hours, the song ends. You look up from your useless sheet music. Dozens of people crowd the CD table. They gaze at you, applauding, and the looks on their faces are more than appreciative—they are adoring, awestruck, rapt. They are flying at the helms of their own personal ships. The fact that you haven't really been playing has made no difference in sales. It's an important realization: Your silence sells music.

But this does not trouble you, not at that moment. Instead, you feel relieved. If no one can hear you play the violin, you won't be fired for being a mediocre violinist. It isn't just about needing

money. You are desperate for something that this job is already giving you, though you wouldn't have been able to say what.

Years later, you will recognize the same desperation in other
young people, especially young women, and you will know: You
were desperate for the respect the customers gave to you as a professional violinist, respect you had never experienced in previous jobs
as a waitress, receptionist, or assistant. In those positions, you acted
flirtatious yet docile. You endured condescension and even harassment by imagining the work was temporary, though it never quite
felt that way. The pose felt intertwined with a more permanent position: female. But playing the violin for money had no such associa-
tions. What you felt that day in New Hampshire was freedom. You
wanted it so badly you didn't dare question whether or not it was real.

God Bless America Tour 2004
Baltimore

"Some people out there have cancer, guys," The Composer says.
This is his nightly preconcert pep talk. He wants us to
smile while we are playing, but we never smile big enough, or con-
tinuously enough. The one exception to this is Harriet, who, as
The Composer tells the audience each night, has "the biggest, most
beautiful smile."

"It's just really important we go out there and smile and touch
their hearts," he continues. "Okay? If we do that, it will be so cool.
So just remember to smile, okay?"

If The Composer is not satisfied with the amount of smiling

during a concert, he speaks to us again after the performance, pleading with us to consider that the audience is full of people who are sick and old and going through horrible pain. These people turn to him, The Composer, for relief. His music allows them to relax and think nice thoughts. How are they going to relax and think nice thoughts if we aren't happy and relaxed and smiling? Objections pertaining to the difficulty of smiling with a violin under one's chin are ignored. The implication is that if we forget to smile, we could kill someone.

To be fair, there is no one more dedicated to smiling during concerts than The Composer himself. But his smile is so forced that only his most stalwart fans are left undisturbed by it. His face freezes into a triangle-shaped rock, his eyebrows arch upward in an unconvincing pantomime of mirth, his lips force their way into a toothy smile that is all hard angles and sharp lines. One of the very few negative reviews of The Composer on Amazon puts it this way: *The nature footage is beautiful but I was distracted by the psychotic grin on the conductor guy.* An unsatisfied viewer on Netflix writes: *I found this video unsettling. The musicians are all smiling too much, as if they've been indoctrinated into a cult.*

After thirty minutes of music, it is time for The Composer's halftime speech. Harriet, Stephen, and I sit down in plastic folding chairs, our instruments resting in our laps.

"I am so very blessed to see you all tonight," he begins, speaking into a live microphone. "We're all just so . . . um . . . grateful . . . blessed you could come."

The official objective of the God Bless America Tour is to help raise money for local PBS stations. During his halftime speech, which, like the music, never changes night after night, The Composer launches into a brief, awkward spiel, preaching to the pledge-drive choir about the wonders of public television. He claims that as a kid he watched PBS programs, that this is what inspired him to become a composer. And then he gets to the story everyone wants to hear, the story about the The A-List Hollywood Celebrity.

"So . . . uh . . . as you know, our God Bless America special is narrated by The Hollywood Celebrity," he begins. "And it was so cool . . . I got to go out to Los Angeles to work with him. So I thought I'd tell you about it."

The Composer's Story About The Hollywood Celebrity is this: The Hollywood Celebrity is a really fun guy. A really cool guy. A really awesome guy who is also really fun. The Hollywood Celebrity rode to the recording studio on a motorcycle. Which was really cool. And fun. But the funnest, coolest thing is that The Hollywood Celebrity cares about PBS. Enough to take time from his glamorous Hollywood life to work with the humble Composer.

The audience is enraptured by this speech, and it *is* quite amazing to think of The Composer and The Hollywood Celebrity in the same room together. I bet they both smiled a lot. Perhaps there was even a smiling contest, and The Hollywood Celebrity discovered that he had finally met his match. But left unmentioned during this speech is that The Hollywood Celebrity, however much he may care about PBS, may have also been motivated to narrate the God Bless America special because The Composer paid him tens of thousands of dollars to record a few minutes of narration.

Also unmentioned during the speech: When it comes to supporting PBS, The Composer is the real superstar. Other than a small trickle of revenue he receives from the CD sales table at the concerts, The Composer is not getting paid by PBS for the tour. The audience members have "won" admission to the concert by pledging donations to their local PBS stations. The money for the

RV and the hotels and our salaries is coming out of The Composer's own pocket.

And it is this fact, more than anything else, that makes him a mysterious figure to me: So much about The Composer—his music, his performances, his smile—is ripped off, imitated, or downright fake. But when it comes to the most genuine gesture an American can make—giving away money—The Composer is the real deal. The profits from his CD sales are spent doing free tours for PBS and producing benefit CDs for charities. On some nights after our concerts, he gives away as many CDs as he sells.

After impressing the audience with stories of The Hollywood Celebrity, there is one last thing The Composer must do before completing the concert.

"On my new CD, *Wildflower Sunrise*, I tried to compose a waltz," he says in his trademark high-pitched whisper, an affected stage voice he uses that sounds half Michael Jackson, half surfer dude. "I thought it would be really cool. And I was wondering . . . um . . . if I gave you this CD for free, would anyone out in the audience like to . . . uh . . . like to waltz with me?"

"I DO!!" screams a woman in the audience. She jumps to her feet with a swiftness inconsistent with her age and hurries to the stage.

The Composer giggles, turns on the CD player. He approaches the woman shyly, as if at an old-timey middle school dance, and suddenly she becomes shy, too. For the next few minutes the audience watches as The Composer waltzes robotically around the stage with an elderly woman. The woman beams up at him, glowing. The Composer never looks straight at her, choosing instead to stare out into the audience, his face contorted into a manic, rigid smile.

For a long time, whenever I saw that smile on The Composer, I kept thinking he looked like someone famous, but I couldn't place who it was. When he's not doing his stage smile, one could say he resembles James Franco, or Jim Morrison, or even a very thin Clark Gable. But during concerts, his fake grin distorts his features. One night I look over at him waltzing with a middle-aged woman and it clicks: The rigid angles at which he holds his head and the unchanging toothiness of his expression give him—an otherwise handsome man—an uncanny resemblance to the velociraptors in *Jurassic Park*.

Years later, I will question this association between The Composer and a deadly yet comic beast. What about him and his musical charade did I fear might rip me apart?

After the waltz, The Composer has one more announcement to make to the crowd before we finish the concert: "I just want you all to know I'm praying for you, praying for you all," he says, smiling the velociraptor smile. "I want you all to stay safe."

Milli Violini

New Hampshire, 2002

"I've heard that they're firing everyone," Debbie says to Yevgeny over a lobster shack dinner on the shore of Alton Bay. "Am I going to be fired?"

"I don't think so," Yevgeny says. "You're here now, aren't you?"

"They're firing people?" you ask.

"Why do you think they hired you?" Debbie asks incredulously, tossing her red hair. "They're getting rid of all the old musicians. The Composer wants fresh young pretty ones like yourself. The old ones were asking too many questions, were starting to raise a stink with the union."

"The union?" you ask.

"Jessica's not in the musician's union," Yevgeny says. "She's a college student."

"You're not a professional musician?" Debbie asks.

"No," you confess, pleased she hadn't been able to tell this about you before. "And I don't even know what type of music we're playing. Is it classical? New Age? Soundtrack music?"

"The genre is called 'Crap,'" Debbie says. "It's got all the popularity of Rap with the respectability of Classical. People love Crap. Can't get enough Crap. The Composer hit #1 on the Crap Billboard list.

"But you're asking the wrong question," she continues, taking a sip of her margarita. "The question you *should* be asking is 'What genre do the customers *think* it is?' The answer to *that* question is classical. Any time a violin and a flute play together live on a stage— voila! It's classical! And Yevgeny here is the perfect picture of a classical violinist—look at him! So Russian! And in his all-black outfit!"

"No," Yevgeny says, rolling his eyes. "Anyways, the customers think it's the *Titanic* soundtrack."

"It *is* the *Titanic* soundtrack," Debbie says. "They were almost sued for copyright infringement."

"Well, now they're being more careful," Yevgeny says. "They keep it just within the legal amount of notes. They just rereleased *Oceans of April* with the notes changed around a bit, just to be safe."

"Who is 'they'?" you ask. "Don't you mean The Composer?"

"The Composer and his helpers," Debbie says with a giggle. "They write the music."

You look at Yevgeny for an explanation but he is scowling at Debbie.

"But doesn't he perform with the New York Philharmonic and on PBS?"

"Everything has a price," Debbie says.

"And the background track is so loud," you say. "I can barely hear the actual sounds of your instruments, especially the violin. Does anyone in the audience ever care about that?"

"Not many. A few," Yevgeny says. "What does it matter? What are they going to do, report us to the music police?"

"So we're like Milli Vanilli," you say. "Like a classical music version of Milli Vanilli."

"You're not the first Ensemble musician to say that," Yevgeny says.

"Milli Violini?" you ask. Debbie laughs.

"Listen," Yevgeny says, annoyed. "Don't ask too many questions on this gig. It's fine with us—but not all the gigs are going to be like this. You'll be with other people, other musicians, and if you say too much, you might not get called for a gig again."

"Okay," you say. "But, do you think I'll even be hired again? I mean, if they're firing people, and I'm not really a professional musician . . ."

"You'll be hired again," Yevgeny says. "Debbie and I will give you our highest recommendation."

Debbie nods. "You know," she says, "you're the perfect person for this job—an amateur posing as the real thing. You know who else is like that?"

God Bless America Tour 2004
Portland, Maine

The Composer is from New England, and the audience members filing into the performance room are his people—staunch Composer fans. Some even remember his very first gigs when he sold his CDs by himself at craft fairs and malls. Because of this, the local Maine PBS station has chosen a special concert venue: the Holden Frost House, a nineteenth-century mansion. Despite the festive atmosphere of a hometown star appearing in a historic venue, the audience members are grim-faced, as if about to attend jury duty instead of a concert.

The Composer, on the other hand, is giddy. Perhaps this is because the flutist, Stephen, has been replaced on the tour by Kim— The Composer's main pennywhistle star and muse. Kim missed the first week of the tour because she couldn't leave her job as a church music director. Kim is petite with reddish-blond hair and the sort of broad, clean-scrubbed New England face that reminds me of the portraits of "The Pilgrims" in my high school history textbook. On the road, she spends her time alternating between The Composer's bedroom and the RV's sofa, where she reads books from the *Left Behind* series, the Evangelical thrillers in which the Rapture saves only the purest, most Protestant Christians while the rest of humanity is "left behind" to suffer hell. As she reads, her fingers trace the gold cross hanging from her neck. Every once in a while she looks up and sees me watching her from my seat in the kitchen, where I write in my journal and reread *Lolita*.

I have never been this far north. The houses in Maine are thick and squat with fake deer and squirrels in the front yards, the road signs marking distances in both miles and kilometers, perhaps to comfort the Canadians who are almost home. The stubby trees hunch toward the gray sky. Some appear to be covered in green felt. They are nothing like the slim Georgia pines we passed a few days ago in Atlanta, their wide branches drinking the sun. Up here it is already autumn, and a few species of trees are spangled yellow and red. We stop at a grocery store and I buy fresh lobster dip and crackers. Everything in Maine feels sharper, crisper. Stark.

By concert time, The Composer is bouncing around the mansion with excitement, greeting stern-faced elderly audience members, shoving fistfuls of Cap'n Crunch into his mouth, leaving a peanut butter-scented cloud of cereal dust in his wake. "Don't forget to smile!" he chirps to me before we walk on stage. He is so excited that halfway through the concert he decides to deviate from his usual midconcert speech about the wonders of PBS and The Story About The Hollywood Celebrity.

But first he lights a long white candle and grips it in his hand, as if at a vigil.

"You know," he begins, "being in this old house really reminds me of the olden times, and like, how romantic it is."

The audience looks back at him, their faces blank.

"In the olden times it was so romantic," he continues. "There were candles." He looks at the candle in his hand as if it will help him understand what he means.

"And you know," he continues, "there were horses and buggies. And slaves."

Harriet and I look at each other. Slaves? Kim shakes her head in embarrassment. But no one in the audience seems bothered that The Composer has just called slavery romantic.

"So Kim and I are going to do something . . . um . . . special for you guys tonight," The Composer continues, smiling the veloci-raptor. Harriet and I look at each other, having no idea what he's talking about but glad that, whatever it is, we seem to have no role in it.

What happens next is as unexpected as his proclamation about slavery being the good old days. For the first time in my career as a musician for The Composer, I witness a truly live performance.

The Composer plays a few chords on his keyboard. He approaches the keys gingerly, making frequent and obvious mistakes with his own composition. It becomes clear why, in the PBS God Bless America special, the camera avoids The Composer's hands.

While The Composer bumbles around on the keyboard, Kim flawlessly toots the simple flute melody. When they are finished, the audience claps politely. But there is a palpable feeling of relief in the room when we return to our usual performance method: playing very softly while the clamor of the CD erases any trace of our real, imperfect sounds.

After the concert, an elderly woman with pinkish hair greets me at the refreshment table where Harriet and I are filling paper cups with strawberry-orange punch.

"You are so talented," she says to me. "Where did you study?"

"I didn't really study," I answer. "I mean, nothing other than lessons."

"But then how did you become a professional?"

"Just a lucky audition," I say.

"You're so modest!"

And then she says something that reminds me of my own olden times: the 1990s.

She says, "You have a real gift."

You Have a Real Gift

Virginia, 1990s

The adults always say this. "You have a real gift." They say "real" like "reeyell."

The West Virginia teachers go on strike and school is canceled indefinitely. Your family responds to this crisis by moving a few mountains across the state line, into rural western Virginia. Your new town is only a few miles from the West Virginia border and is still within the Appalachian mountains, still a place where chicken processing is a top industry. But the culture of your new town is different, more Shenandoah Valley sunshine and southern hospitality than holler darkness and mountaintop isolation. With the move, the accents of the people around you change from hillbilly to Southern hillbilly. The conflict over slavery called the Civil War becomes the conflict over "states' rights" called "The War between the States." And your violin lessons, once hours and mountains away, are now just a thirty-minute cruise up the interstate. With your clothes no longer covered in chicken crumbs and baby vomit, the mountain fog of your early childhood receding into memory, your violin skills improve exponentially. The adults in your new town take note.

They say, "You have a reeyell gift."

They say, "If you keep practicing, you're going to be famous."

They say, "Don't stop practicing like I did."

They say, "You'll get a scholarship for college with a gift like that." (The same line they use with the boys who are good at sports.)

You are only eleven years old but you already know you don't have a reeyell gift, at least not in the way that the townsfolk mean it. If you have a gift, it's the gift of parents willing and able to pay for your violin and lessons and to drive you over the mountaintops to get them, a gift more practical than celestial, more akin to a Dodge minivan than to a fiery-winged angel of music. But you are not *gifted*. You are not a prodigy.

Your parents know this, too. When people tell them, "Jessica has a reeyell gift," your parents smile politely and respond, "Jessica works very hard."

It's true. You work very hard. A teacher writes on your report card: "Jessica possesses an exceptional work ethic." Years later, the writer Malcolm Harris will articulate the ways in which people of your generation were taught to value work as an end in itself, rather than a process through which something tangible is gained. "When students are working," he writes of the typical millennial classroom experience, "what they're working on is their own ability to work."

But at eleven years old you don't pause to question the work ethic. You simply see what you need to do to be valued in the world around you—work hard—and decide that you will do it better than anyone else. Like any good worker, you have goals and benchmarks. Your goal is to be the best at everything and the most liked by everyone. You are one of the fastest runners in the fifth grade, one of the few girls who can do pull-ups. There isn't a single school subject you don't like. You have plenty of friends who invite you to birthday parties and sleepovers. You are voted vice president of the middle school student council. You're the only kid in school who can play the violin. Fourteen boys ask you to the fifth-grade Valentine's Day Dance, including a set of twins.

You don't know it, but these are the last moments of the brief courtship you get to have with yourself as a female human being in

1990s America, a courtship in which you do not "love yourself" or "hate yourself" (because those terms would not have made sense to you) but instead have a profound sense of satisfaction with the world around you and your apparent role in it.

Then something happens to you.

It's not a single-event trauma. Your parents do not get divorced. No one dies. You are not abused.

And yet. Something happens to you. And because you cannot trace what happens to you to a single, traumatic event, you struggle to explain it, struggle for years to admit that anything happened to you at all.

But it did. It's obvious, visible in your face, your posture. A friend in middle school tells you that her mom has asked her, "What happened to Jessica?"

What happened to you? It's a big fish of a question, large and slippery.

When you are twelve years old, a book titled *Reviving Ophelia: Saving the Selves of Adolescent Girls* becomes a national best-seller. The author, Mary Pipher, writes, "Something dramatic happens to girls in early adolescence. Just as planes and ships disappear mysteriously into the Bermuda Triangle, so do the selves of girls go down in droves." Pipher argues that while adolescence has always been a difficult transition for boys and girls alike, there is something in the cultural air of the early 1990s that has spawned an epidemic of depression, self-mutilation, and eating disorders.

What's curious about this epidemic is that its adolescent female victims are middle class. They come from stable, loving households and have attentive parents. Even stranger is that, as people say in the 1990s, *It's the nineties!*, meaning, "women are equal now." A teacher tells your class, "You can be anything you want if you work hard enough," and then adds, "This is true for girls now, too." What no one ever says during your entire upbringing is that there has been a cultural price to pay for equality, a counterattack aiming its weapons at your fast-developing female body. The counterattack goes by various names—*Backlash* by Susan Faludi or *The Beauty Myth* by Naomi Wolf, who in 1991 writes, "These little girls, born around the time of Ronald Reagan's first election, are showing third-generation mutations from the beauty backlash against the women's movement. . . . This generation will have more trouble with life in the body than do daughters of the 1960s and 1970s."

What strikes you reading Wolf's words now, as a person born two months after Reagan's first inauguration, is Wolf's phrase *life in the body*, a phrase that separates the theoretical potential of femaleness in the age of equality from the actual, lived reality of it. Born into the first generation of girls whose political and civic equality was already assumed, you are told from the earliest age that you can become an astronaut, a doctor, the president of the United States (if you work hard enough). The potential for your life supposedly has no bounds. But by your twelfth birthday, you have a sinking feeling. You can't do life in this body. Not *this* body, the one that is appearing slowly, then suddenly before you in the mirror. This body is a stranger; you don't know it, you don't like it. It's certainly not the body you would have ordered from a catalog. You have a new vision of yourself, a vision of what you are actually going to look like as a woman. And in that vision—a short-legged, big-thighed brunette with monstrous eyebrows and a crooked smile—you no longer see a place for yourself in the world.

Indeed, you no longer see a place for yourself in the seventh grade. The talents that a short time ago won you admiration from your friends, the winsome qualities that led the fourteen boys including the set of twins to ask you to the dance, have become irrelevant. No matter how hard you work, you find yourself sliding down the social hierarchy, while other girls—quiet, skinny, pretty (*impossibly pretty*, a phrase from *Teen* magazine, which you have recently begun reading, devouring its beauty tips)—are making their ascent. By the middle of seventh grade you are friendless and under a daily torrent of teasing by a pack of boys. Several teachers notice your suffering and their response is universal: "Those boys just like you." But even then you know that this is profoundly untrue. Those boys do not like you. Those boys have sniffed out your growing insecurity and have pounced on it. *It's the nineties!* Those boys—victims of the backlash themselves—are becoming more aware by the day that girls are a commodity, like livestock, to be traded with other boys, and that your value is in a period of deflation.

You say nothing of any of this to your parents, though your mom senses it. After one particularly hard week in which you are not invited to a crucial birthday party, she takes you out of seventh grade for a day so that the two of you can make the four-hour round trip journey to the National Gallery in Washington, D.C. Once there, you gaze upon the gruesome *Watson and the Shark*, painted by John Singleton Copley in 1778. The shark's open jaws are frozen in time, inches away from Watson's blond head, his face contorted in agony, his severed limb a dark absence in the water. When you return to look at the painting as an adult, you notice the terror and helplessness of the two people on the boat, whose faces are obscured, their arms outstretched. They are so close to Watson but can't reach him; their hands clutch the air around his torso. Watson is so busy looking at the oncoming shark that he can't see their efforts, doesn't realize how far they are reaching out to save him.

Best-selling how-to-save-Ophelia books aside, was it even possible for any parent of a daughter in the early 1990s to do much but watch from the boat as an entire generation of girls sank beneath the surface? After your trip to the gallery, you and your mom stop at a café for French onion soup. She tries to give you words of encouragement, words to help you navigate what she imagines to be the typically treacherous waters of middle school drama. You can't bring yourself to tell her the real problem: You aren't pretty enough. You will *never* be pretty enough. You can't tell her because you are ashamed that you have a problem so clearly unfixable, a problem that can't be solved by working harder. Everywhere you look—magazines, TV, movies, high school pep rallies—you see that not being pretty enough will mean your life will be much different—more difficult, more restricted—than you would have ever imagined a few years before. And even if you somehow did become beautiful, you know it would not be enough to put you on equal footing with the boys.

One bleak night, a few months before your thirteenth birthday, you sneak out your bedroom window and walk a mile through a snowstorm to the interstate overpass near your house. You intend to jump off of it, and you spend minutes willing yourself to lean farther and farther over the railing. But after a while you back off and lie down in the snow, listening to the scream of the eighteen-wheelers as they fly beneath your body. The interstate is the biggest difference between your old town in West Virginia and your new one in Virginia. The noise of the traffic on it reverberates off the mountainsides, a hymn of American commerce that brings goods you had never encountered in West Virginia: granola bars, flavored tea, live lobsters.

"I know what you must be thinking," says Kate Winslet's Rose after her suicide attempt in *Titanic*. " 'Poor little rich girl. What does she know about misery?' "

"No," Jack responds compassionately. "What I was thinking was, what could have happened to this girl to think she had no way out?"

Life in the body.

By high school, the anorexia epidemic spreads its tentacles into the bodies and/or minds of almost every girl you know. It creeps into town and stalks its victims; girls collapse on the gymnasium floor, on the running track, in the shower. They are scraped off floors and lawns and bathtubs, shipped off to the hospital, then to rehab. There are whispers of "heart attack," "force-feeding," "nose tube." There are louder conversations about what techniques those girls used and how to best emulate them for one's own purposes. In the cafeteria, tables of girls dump canisters of black pepper onto their lunches in collective rituals of self-imposed refusal.

The adults are incredulous. They don't seem to recognize the epidemic, or at least, they don't see how large the presence is, how menacing. How it doesn't just manifest physically, but psychologically. Famine, to them, is something last brought about by Sherman's March of ransacking Yankees. Famine is *not* something willed into existence by a bunch of silly teenage girls who are so *ungrateful* for the opportunities girls have now. *It's the nineties!* Don't we know that girls can be anything they want to be if they work hard enough?

What we want to be is skeletal. By fifteen your body is begging you for calories, to let yourself grow. You are losing weight instead, your work ethic turned inward, toward your own flesh, which you are convinced you can eviscerate. *All you need to do is work hard!* You don't succeed. But girls who lack the genes or the willpower to fully commit to starvation, yourself included, don't give up trying. There are many differences between girls with full-blown anorexia and those who can't quite squeeze themselves into the disease, but self-hatred is not one of them. An inability to reconcile *life in the body* is not one of them. You survive for a week on water and a single sour, green Jolly Rancher. You try ipecac syrup and diet pills. You join sports teams not because they bring you pleasure (you hate sports) but because you hope they will shrink your muscular body to a stick. You wake up at dawn for weight-lifting class, drink a single cup of coffee, skip lunch, go to track or cross-country or soccer practice, and arrive home at night light-headed and morose. Your mom makes spaghetti and meatballs. You gobble down two plates. And the failure of this—*two plates of spaghetti, you disgusting pig!*—weighs on you more than any other failure.

But unlike so many of the other drowning girls, you have something tethering you to the shore. When you play the violin, you are told you have a reeyell gift. That's bullshit, you have no gift, but there's something about the way that people look at you when you're playing. (As a teenage girl, you are a world-class expert—a veritable PhD in visual semantics—on the subject of the facial expressions of people who are looking at you.) When you put your violin under your chin, there is a brief moment in which your worth as a human being is not being gauged on a scale of relative beauty (*her face is a six, but her ass is a ten*). When you play the violin you are able, for a moment, to leave the female body in which you are contained, the body that signals sex, whether you want it to or not, yet is somehow never sexy enough. By putting a violin under your chin—or even carrying a violin case through the puke-green corridors of your high school—it is as if you're telling the world that you have authority on something, and in having this authority, you are more complex, more consequential than your young female body suggests.

For the most enraging aspect of *life in the body* isn't that you aren't skinny or sexy enough, it's that *life in the body* causes you to be dismissed as silly and shallow and stupid in a way that boys who are equally silly and shallow and stupid are not. Playing classical music on the violin provides a corrective: The violin is serious. Classical music is serious. An understanding of classical music—something adults say they wish they knew more about but don't—gives a girl weight in a world that wants her to be weightless, gives her substance in a culture that asks her to be insubstantial.

And this, it turns out, is the reeyell gift: It is almost as if, by attaching a violin to your body, you can become a dude.

But Why Is Playing the Violin the Cultural Equivalent of Growing a Penis?

In late 1993, when you are twelve years old and just building the stamina to play full-length violin concertos, researchers at the University of California at Irvine have thirty-six college students do a series of geometric puzzles after ten minutes of listening to Mozart's Sonata for Two Pianos in D Major. The students' spatial reasoning IQ scores are eight points higher after listening to Mozart. In the report on this research—a mere three paragraphs published in *Nature*—the researchers warn that the IQ boost only lasts ten to fifteen minutes and that there is no reason to assume that Mozart's music, in particular, has special qualities: "Because we used only one musical sample of one composer, various other compositions and musical styles should also be examined." This caveat will be ignored. "The Mozart Effect" has been born.

The UC Irvine study goes viral in pre-Internet America. The *New York Times* exclaims: "Mozart Makes the Brain Hum." *Time* magazine reports: "Listening to Mozart makes students smarter." Music teachers across the country brandish the UC Irvine study like a shield, fending off budget slashes. The Mozart study is "scientific evidence" that music class improves standardized test scores. "Beethoven is no longer the world's greatest composer," declares Alex Ross in a 1994 *New York Times* article. "Mozart is the composer who gives you an edge on the SATs." By 1997, when Don Campbell publishes his popular book *The Mozart Effect*, the actual results of the UC Irvine study have been left far behind. Campbell compares Mozart to Jesus and claims that listening to Mozart's music not only increases intelligence but also cures everything from brain hemorrhages to autism to paralysis to cancer. Mozart can make cows produce more milk, reduce traffic accidents, and prevent premature birth. Mozart's music can even make yeast rise faster, producing better sake at a brewery in Japan.

The Mozart Effect gains traction during the same era in which Tipper Gore wages war on rap music, the same era in which school dances in the whitest enclaves of Appalachia begin to blend Garth Brooks with Snoop Dogg, whose *Doggystyle* album debuts at number one on the Billboard charts just a few weeks after the Mozart study is published. At your middle school, the boys who hate you grind up against your body to the beat of "Snoop Doggy Doo-oww-ohhh-oggg!" The sexual ministrations of inner-city lyricists become the lingua franca of your generation, fluently spoken by every thirteen-year-old kid regardless of race, class, or geographical location. Decades later, these songs will seem so tame that people will play them at wedding receptions, white grandmas shaking it to Biggie Smalls. But in the early 1990s, the Tipper Gore generation maligns rap and hip-hop as cultural poison. The Mozart Effect offers an antidote; it is "proof," after all, that "good," IQ-enhancing music is composed by old white men, not by young black ones.

But dozens of subsequent studies fail to replicate even the minor increases in IQ achieved in the original study. Most of these follow-up studies conclude that any music that puts the test taker in a better mood increases his test score. So if it is 1993 and you are a thirteen-year-old looking to increase your IQ, you should probably listen to ten minutes of *Doggystyle*.

While the actual effect of listening to Mozart while taking a test is minimal at best, the effect of the UC Irvine study on American culture—The Effect of the Mozart Effect, one could call it, or the Mozart Effect Effect—is tremendous and undeniable. The Mozart Effect Effect thrives in a realm that is neither science nor art, a realm that is far more organically American: marketing. Megacorporations like "Baby Einstein" are born and flourish by promoting the disproven belief that blasting Mozart toward a baby—or even a fetus—can fast-track the kid to Harvard. In 1998, Georgia governor Zell Miller allocates over $100,000 in state funds to provide every child born in Georgia with a tape or CD of classical music, arguing that it will help Georgia's kids outperform their peers in math and science. When a Georgia state legislator asks about the possibility of including Charlie Daniels on the tape, he is told that "classical music has a greater positive impact." The subsequent studies suggest the opposite; Charlie Daniels (likely to put more Georgians in a good mood) would have been the more productive choice.

At about the same time that every baby in Georgia is receiving a free Mozart tape in the mail, you are engaging in your own misguided attempts to harness the Mozart Effect, having been indoctrinated by school music teachers that the Effect is real and significant.

You listen to the depressing chords of Mozart's *Requiem* during the forty-five-minute drive to the closest SAT test site.

But, of course, the real effect from Mozart in your life comes not from any enhancement to your IQ but from the fact that Americans increasingly believe in the tangible benefits of classical music, while simultaneously knowing less and less about the art form. In the 1990s, classical music becomes both more desirable and more mysterious, a potent combination. Hollywood movies of the 1990s are full of messages about the inherent redemptive and beneficial qualities of classical music: A gal might be a high school dropout and a prostitute, but if she cries for joy during an opera performance, she is inherently upper class and deserves to marry a millionaire (*Pretty Woman*). White women moving to Harlem might mean gentrification, but white women teaching black children classical music equals redemption (*Music of the Heart*). An emotionally distant father having a quasi-affair with a high school student redeems himself by bringing classical music to his deaf son (*Mr. Holland's Opus*). A debilitating mental illness is surmountable, even charming, if one can play Rachmaninoff with enough sweaty passion (*Shine*). Taking away a woman's piano is tantamount to taking away her ability to speak (*The Piano*). A violin is not a mere musical instrument but the body and the blood, the dead Madonna and her dead baby, the corpse of the beloved, the orphan, the gypsy soul, the fuck object, the ultimate weapon against communism, the "perfect marriage of science and beauty" (*The Red Violin*).

In the last paragraph of the original UC Irvine study, the authors speculate that the change in IQ they observed might not be due to an increase from listening to Mozart, the experiment's variable, but instead a *decrease* in IQ from listening to the experiment's control: overly simplified and repetitive relaxation music.

Music like The Composer's.

They write, "We predict that music lacking complexity or which is repetitive may interfere with, rather than enhance, abstract reasoning."

God Bless America Tour 2004
Durham, New Hampshire

The Composer mugs in front of Harriet's video camera.

"Are you trying to capture the sounds, the sights, the smells of a hard-working rock and roll band?" he asks in a fake British accent.

"Hard-working rock and roll what?" Harriet repeats, confused.

He ignores her and continues with his act. "I jaust wont teh say one li'el thing," he says, his British accent slipping into Australian. His eyes widen the same way they do during his real speeches at the concerts. "That the music we try to play for people really resonates with the outer . . ."

"Limits?" Harriet prompts.

"No," The Composer says in the voice of a BBC commentator. "I say it's more like the paint on the walls, it resonates, it resonates . . . It's the pigment in the paint that I try to capture, the salt pieces, the crystal. But if you can get past that, suddenly you open everyone's hearts. It's the pigment."

"Someone's been sniffing paint pigment," Harriet says.

But later, we'll realize what The Composer is talking about: He's imitating the British accents of the band members in *This Is Spinal*

Tap, Christopher Guest's brilliant fake documentary about a fake rock band. Which, it turns out, happens to be The Composer's favorite movie.

After our concert, The Composer has a surprise for all of us. We're going to love it, he says. He tells us to wait in the RV while he sprints off somewhere. We're parked near the college where The Composer studied music and, as Yevgeny once told me, played in a hair metal band.

"What was the name of the band?" I had asked Yevgeny.

"I don't know, but they tried to do the same thing we do—play at malls and craft fairs and sell CDs. It doesn't work for heavy metal."

"Yeah, I can see how there might be a few problems with that," I said.

"And then he tried doing children's music," Yevgeny said.

"The Pirate video?"

"Yeah, and that didn't work; I think he just freaked kids out. And then he did Irish music for a while, but that's an oversaturated market. And then nature sounds."

"And then *Titanic*."

"Yeah," Yevgeny said. "And that's what sells."

Patrick, Harriet, Kim, and I wait for The Composer outside the RV in the chilly afternoon air. Harriet has announced that tonight she's going to try to make us all okra soup using the RV's stove, though anytime someone cooks, we all worry about being poisoned with oven gas, or, even worse, the RV exploding into a fireball on the freeway. But it is soup weather, and comforting homemade soup seems worth the risk. The sunlight is slanted; the air has a singed-leaf smell.

The Composer sprints back, carrying a box. He is wearing his concert clothes with his running sneakers.

"You guys!" he yells as he approaches. "I have something for you! They shipped it here from the office. You're gonna love it!"

He sets the box on the ground and starts pulling out the contents: large piles of black felt. The cloth unfolds to reveal large black varsity jackets with leather sleeves, the kind athletes pin their medals on in high school. The first jacket goes to Patrick, who puts it on and models it for us. As he turns around, we see that the back is embroidered in white cursive letters: *God Bless America Tour 2004*. (Long after the rest of us have stealthily shoved our jackets into the RV's cargo hold, Patrick will proudly wear his, even in the hottest weather. Patrick loves his jacket so much that The Composer orders him several official God Bless America Tour 2004 polo shirts to wear with it.)

Once all of us are in our jackets, The Composer takes a photograph.

"We look like a real tour now," he says. "We look like real musicians."

God Bless America Tour 2004
Norfolk, Virginia

The Composer runs along the beach, the tide of the Atlantic lapping at his sneakers. I sit on a hotel towel in the sand, watching him and writing in my journal. Looking through the pages that I've written so far, I see that they are full of anecdotes of The Composer's bizarre behavior. He broils a cake that ends up in a trash can. He only eats apples and mashed-up Cap'n Crunch cereal. He doesn't recognize Beethoven's Fifth Symphony. He waltzes. He runs laps in his concert clothes. He orders us ridiculous jackets. He smiles like a velociraptor and becomes aggravated when he feels we are not smiling enough. His favorite line from the movie *Spinal Tap* is "It's such a fine line between stupid and clever."

But so what? Why do I care so much? I'm not interested in exposing his "fraud," if that's even what it could be called, to the world. I'm not keeping my journal as some part of an undercover investigation.

I look out onto the Atlantic. There's something else. Something more here. Something bigger about The Composer and his music. Something I'm missing. Something I have to keep going in order to find.

I use my journal to do some God Bless America Tour math: 2 months, 3,000 miles, 37 cities, and 27 concerts from now I will reach the Pacific.

PART II

Asea

If you put a musical instrument in a kid's hand, he or she will never pick up a gun.

—Dr. José Antonio Abreu, founder of Venezuela's internationally acclaimed Youth Orchestra program

The fact is, I can't fool you, any one of you. It simply isn't fair to you or me. The worst crime I can think of would be to rip people off by faking it and pretending as if I'm having 100% fun. Sometimes I feel as if I should have a punch-in time clock before I walk out on stage. I've tried everything within my power to appreciate it (and I do, God, believe me I do, but it's not enough). I appreciate the fact that I and we have affected and entertained a lot of people.

—Kurt Cobain, in his suicide note

God Bless America Tour 2004
Charlotte to Jacksonville

We sail into the whirling hem of Hurricane Charley, rain and wind buffeting the sides of the RV. We are under a tornado watch and I search the skies. Kim reads her *Left Behind* book, her Pilgrim face unconcerned with mortal peril, secure in Jesus. Harriet finds solace in her headphones, listening to an odd mix that she describes as therapeutic: Digable Planets, Jefferson Starship, and Barbra Streisand. The Composer sits in the front with Patrick and rolls down the passenger-side window. He sticks his head out into the hurricane's stinging rain, looking backward at the road already traveled. His tongue hangs out of his mouth slightly and he wears the same expression that dogs do when they hang their heads out of car windows. The expression that says, *This is great!*

Late at night, when I'm in bed and Harriet is still awake watching TV (she likes MTV's *The Real World: Philadelphia*), I try to read *On the Road*, because that's the book I think I should be reading. But I can't get into it, maybe because by page three some guy is already telling a female character to make breakfast and sweep the floor and calling her a whore. The same guy name-drops Schopenhauer into casual conversation, and the narrator thinks this guy is the coolest. I have no patience for this bullshit, not now, not while actually on the American road. And so I try to go to sleep but the TV is too loud. I begin to put a pillow on my face each night in an attempt to muffle *The Real World*.

The Composer doesn't eat meals after noon, and he works all night in the RV composing the Christian musical—or "worship and praise music," as Kim calls it—for some small-town theater. This poses a problem: the rest of us are hungry—we want to eat supper. But we are confined to whatever restaurants are within walking distance of the hotel. And because our hotels are usually Hampton Inns or Howard Johnsons or Ramada Limiteds in suburban strip malls (because these are the easiest places to park an RV), our meals have a depressing similarity to them, whether we are in Maine or in Maryland or in Georgia.

"This entire nation is a goddamn Ruby Tuesday," I write in an email back home to friends (Subject: RV There Yet?). I am becoming agitated with the monotonous landscape of suburban sprawl. I am "in a despair," as my mom would call it. We are in rural Georgia and I want it to feel like rural Georgia. I want to go to a local diner where a woman named Pam calls me "Honey" and serves me up a fresh slice of homemade peach pie. Instead, I'm at a Ruby Tuesday. I'm eating something called Louisiana shrimp. I can taste the microwaves still radiating off of it, and anyway, I don't want Louisiana shrimp in Georgia because I can have Louisiana shrimp when we get to goddamned Louisiana. I want peach pie. I want sweet tea. I want Pam.

And music is being piped into the Ruby Tuesday dining room, an endless loop of rock music, offensive in its innocuousness. I become alarmed that this music has been hand selected by corporate executives at Ruby Tuesday's headquarters in an elaborate psycho-musical ploy to get me to buy an extra appetizer, but perhaps I am overly sensitive to the dangers of elaborate psycho-musical ploys. I hurl curses at Harriet and Kim.

"I didn't go on this goddamned tour to see every goddamned Ruby Tuesday in America," I huff, stabbing at a stiff shrimp.

"Do you want some of my ribs?" Harriet asks.

"No, I want to see America," I say.

"This is it," Kim says.

New York City
1999

After you inject yourself with the hormones—a small needle in the top of your thigh and a large needle in the side of your butt cheek, each shot given twice per day—you drop the spent syringes into an empty Sunny Delight bottle so they won't stab the dormitory janitors. Your freshman roommate, Ariel, eyes the syringe-filled bottle, along with the black and blue bruises ballooning on your body, with increasing alarm and disgust. In addition to the usual things freshmen roommates have to negotiate to get along, Ariel has an additional challenge: How to handle a roommate from Appalachia who is clueless about everything from city life to hip-hop music to the canon of Western literature. A roommate who wears clothes that border on corporate business attire because prior to arriving in New York her idea of what New Yorkers wore each day came from newsreels of bankers walking down Wall Street. A roommate who is so desperate for tuition money that within just a few weeks of arriving in New York City, she has answered an advertisement in the college newspaper (Help a woman become a mother! Earn $5,000!) and become an egg donor.

Having no concept of your parents' finances, you have no idea why you haven't qualified for more financial aid. It will be a decade before you understand what really happened, because it is only then that it becomes a national news story: Your parents, who were loving, generous, and fiscally responsible, saved for their three children's college tuitions for years, only to find out that you, the oldest kid, could deplete the entire savings account with a few semesters in the Ivy League. Because this was 1999, years before the tuition crisis garnered media attention, no one in your family realized that the same problem was about to be faced by the entire middle class, even the upper-middle class, and not just at private universities but at state schools as well.

Your parents begged you to turn down Columbia and go somewhere cheaper. But you were determined. You had a semester's worth of scholarship aid and you could take out the maximum in federal student loans. With the money your parents had saved for you to go to state school added to the mix, all you needed to do was earn around $8,000 per semester, plus living expenses. You could do that, you told them with confidence, figuring that in New York City, anything was possible.

"Why Columbia, is what I want to know," your dad said in April of your senior year, the deadline to send a tuition deposit days away. "Until Fernando got in, who had ever heard of the place? Do you know anyone who would pay that much for a kid's college education? Besides Fernando's parents?"

Fernando was your high school boyfriend. His Jewish, bira-cial, New York City–native parents had moved to your town a few years earlier for reasons unclear to everyone; your rural Appa-lachian town was not known for welcoming the non-Christian or the nonwhite. It was a town in which even you, with your Italian heritage, were seen as foreign, your black hair marking you an obvious outsider, a teacher describing you as "urban" in a recommendation letter even though you'd never lived in a town with more than three thousand people. When Fernando had his bar mitzvah, the local Hallmark had no bar mitzvah cards, so they ordered one box and everyone in town gave Fernando the same card. But for whatever reason, Fernando's family had chosen your town, and in doing so they changed your own geo-graphical destiny. For it was Fernando who introduced you to the Northeast, a region that you had hitherto thought about only in literary terms, in eleventh-grade English class, as you dissected nineteenth-century transcendentalist poems. *Till the gossamer thread you fling, catch somewhere.* All of these poems seemed to involve snow, or death, or death by freezing in the snow. The works of Hawthorne, Emerson, Thoreau, Whitman, Dickenson, and Frost were all cut from the same ice cube: The Northeast, as you imagined it, was a society of neo-Pilgrims who spent long winters contemplating God, looking for their souls in a spider-web, philosophizing on boring, uncontroversial subjects. You much preferred the fiery Louisiana nights of Robert Penn War-ren, the biscuit-hot Arkansas of Maya Angelou, the rabid Ever-glades of Zora Neale Hurston.

Until you began dating Fernando in the eleventh grade and trav-eled to New York City with his family, it never occurred to you that the Northeast was a region of outsize importance. You had no clue that the Northeast was—150 years after the transcendentalists—still the place to go if you were young and aspiring to one day become a contributor to American literature, music, or art (not to mention politics, science, and finance). Before you met Fernando, you had no idea that the Northeast was the place where rich important people determine what the rest of the country will read and listen to and think about. You were under the mistaken impression—common among rural teenagers outside of the Northeast—that American culture was like American land, underneath everyone's feet, available for anyone to cultivate and harvest.

But all of that changed with Fernando. He was a year older than you. His parents had sent him hours away to a private school near D.C. for his elementary and middle school years. At your public high school, he became the first person ever to be accepted to an Ivy League university: Columbia. Fernando's parents were the only people in town who thought highly enough of Columbia to be indignant when you were accepted a year later ("How did *she* get in?" his parents asked).

During Fernando's first year he called you long distance on his dormitory phone to brag about his life in New York City, from the art museums he visited ("Do you know anything about da Vinci? Of course you don't") to the concerts he attended at Lincoln Center ("So I just met Yo-Yo Ma." *You met him?* "Well, I saw him." *That's so cool!*) to the opportunities for employment ("I just made $200 modeling for Dockers khakis." *Wow!*) to what he was reading ("Having Kenneth Koch as a poetry professor makes me realize how bad our education system is in Virginia. Do you know 'Leaves of Grass'?" *Is that one of the Pilgrim poets?* "No, it's Walt Whitman. Like the most important American poet ever. Jesus, Jess") to the food ("I ate sushi last night with this guy Dan who is Korean but speaks fluent Mandarin and is a chef at Nobu. He's actually from California. His major is Russian literature . . ." *Isn't sushi raw fish?* "Jesus, Jess. You're an idiot"). And so you became determined to go to New York City, too. Perhaps living there would inoculate you against future accusations of idiocy, cleanse the cow pie stench of countrified ignorance that Fernando smelled on you. Though your teachers and parents worried that you were following Fernando, whom everyone, including you, knew was a profligate cheater, the truth was that he was no longer the point of the operation, only the means by which you could gain information about an inaccessible world that now seemed crucial to your future.

As you inject yourself with the egg-stimulating hormones, you tell yourself, with a teenager's self-importance, that you have only one chance at this, the elite Northeast. You will do whatever it takes. You know that many people you grew up with were smarter than you, more naturally gifted, and yet they won't be given this chance, or any chance at all. Most of them are not at college but in the military or working—at the chicken plant, Walmart, the truck stop. You aren't about to squander this rare lucky break, this once-in-a-lifetime opportunity.

But just two months into your freshman year of college, you lie on the cool tile floor of your dorm in a warm puddle of your own green vomit, a side effect of ovarian hyperstimulation syndrome. The egg donation process has distracted and sickened you to the point that you have failed all of your midterms. Your roommate, Ariel, who studied cello at Julliard precollege, has won the prestigious university-wide concerto competition, has won it as a freshman. You have failed to make last chair of the student orchestra.

Your violin professor—an Eastern European woman who screams *Calm down!* while you're playing, and asks, *Why are you playing like that? So exaggerated! So loud! Are you trying to make everyone hear your mistakes more clearly?*— has suggested that her time would be better spent hammering nails into her forehead than it would be teaching you how to play the violin.

And of all the failures that you contemplate as you lie on your dorm floor retching out green bile—your midterms, your relationship with Fernando (which never made it past the first week of classes), your inability to blend in with the other students (who go out for drinks in the East Village while you set your alarm for dawn and then take a crosstown bus to a Madison Avenue fertility clinic)—it is this, your failure at the violin, that is most painful. You are beginning to realize, with a certainty you never had to face while growing up in a small town and being told you had "a reeyell gift," that you will never make a living as a violinist. Despite everything your family did to get you an instrument, to get you over the mountains to a violin teacher, despite ten years of lessons and practice and orchestra rehearsals and music camp and your real, true, genuine, passionate, heart-brimming love for the sound of violin music, music that you played in your head for years to stave off mountain fog, it's all come to this: You simply aren't good enough, and you never will be.

And if you aren't a violinist—you who clung to your violin like it was a life preserver, like a prosthetic phallus, like a shield and a sword with which you battled the feeling that you were just an average-looking, unsubstantial, nothing-special girl, a girl who could be thrown under the bus of American culture with all the other girls—then who are you?

What You Wish You Could Tell the Girl Lying in Green Vomit

Ariel, you will find out years after college graduation, hated playing the cello. Her Julliard teachers were abusive. One called Ariel "fat" every time she missed a note. Another threw a music stand across the room during one of her lessons. "It was psychological torture," she will tell you, and you will be shocked because it had seemed like Ariel loved playing the cello. But you had mistaken her success for happiness, which turns out not to be the same thing. After she won the concerto competition, Ariel stopped playing her cello.

And you—a violinist who couldn't play all the high notes, who didn't make the cut for the college orchestra, whose college violin teacher expressed a desire to fill her ear canals with cement rather than hear another note you produced—you will spend half of your twenties touring the country and the world as a professional violinist.

And yet even this success—for that is what, at the beginning at least, you will think it is: an unqualified, simple triumph that you could write home to Appalachia about—will reshape itself in your mind, until you see it as something less like a trophy or a prize and more like a long, circuitous road in which the intended destination disappears upon arrival. An imperfect journey that nonetheless yields unexpected rewards. What you wish you could tell the girl lying in the green vomit is this: The least talented violinist in the orchestra—the one in the last chair of the back row—gets to sit closest to the drums.

Mall Music

2002

Yevgeny and Debbie's recommendation must have worked because a few days after your first gig in New Hampshire Becca Belge calls to ask whether you can work the following weekend. And this time, instead of a seller-trainee, you'll be working as a violinist.

"Who will I be working with?" you ask.

"The awesomest person in the whole Ensemble," Becca says.

"Who is that?"

"Me."

Becca, it turns out, is almost as new to The Composer's Ensemble as you are. As assistant production manager, she hires musicians, schedules gigs, and books travel and lodging for The Composer and his multiple groups of roving minstrels (you later find out there are as many as twelve "Ensembles" working at a time, so that concerts may be "performed" at multiple craft fairs and malls on any given weekend). The head production manager, Jake, thinks Becca might benefit from going on a weekend gig where she can learn the ins and outs of the business while selling CDs. And so you meet Becca at the office on the Upper West Side and begin the journey to the concert venue: a shopping mall in Natick, Massachusetts.

Becca is tall with a cherubic face and bobbed hair dyed a punk shade of red. She jams herself into the driver's seat of the rental car without bothering to adjust it for her height and slams the door. The car feels much smaller and hotter with her inside it.

"Look at this!" she instructs you, throwing a scrap of paper into your lap. It appears to have directions scribbled on it, but you can't make out a single word. "Do you know where we're going?"

You stare at her for a moment, thinking she must be pulling your leg. She isn't.

"Not exactly," you say apologetically. "But I have a pretty good sense of direc—"

"Motherfucker!"

You freeze, but she isn't yelling at you. She is yelling at the car stereo, which is rejecting her CD. With a forceful shove, she finally gets the CD to go in and twirls the volume dial to full blast.

"Do you like AC/DC?" she asks.

"WHAT?"

"DO YOU LIKE AC/DC?"

"YEAH I GUESS!" you answer, reaching to turn down the volume.

"Badass. I've also got Eminem." She waves the rapper's CD close to your face. Becca hits the gas and your head hits the back of the seat. You are off.

"I don't like using mirrors so I'm gonna need you to tell me what's going on," Becca says as she accelerates onto Interstate 95, taking both hands off the wheel to light a cigarette.

"Okay," you reply.

"Can I get over now?" she asks.

"No."

Becca takes a deep drag of her cigarette. "Do you know what this song is about?"

You have never listened closely to AC/DC. Becca cranks up the volume and begins to shout along:

Dirty deeds and they're done dirt cheap
Dirty deeds and they're done dirt cheap

"It's about a group of assassins in Vietnam," Becca says. "Can I get over?"

"No . . . wait!" The car swerves in and out of the lane.

"Or maybe it was Russia. Anyway, they torture people. Torture 'em for money."

"But not very much money," you add helpfully.

"Right," Becca says, smiling at you.

Despite her lack of skill with the rearview mirror, Becca is a virtuoso of the car horn—she plays it frequently and with passion. Every few minutes she adds a vocal element to the performance, sticking her head out the window to yell lyrical renditions of the word "motherfucker" at the Connecticut moms in SUVs.

Even though Yevgeny and Debbie warned you not to ask questions, you are dying to hear Becca's thoughts on The Composer, his music, and the nature of the gig. But when you ask her what The Composer is like, she becomes uncharacteristically quiet.

"He's a sweetheart," she says. And for the first time all day her eyes are locked on the road.

"Do you like the music?" you ask.

"Yeah. It's nice."

"Does The Composer work with you in the office?"

"No—he works at the New England office," Becca says. "I've actually only met him once."

"The New England office?"

"Can I get over?" she asks, veering into the next lane.

"Um . . . no."

Six hours and a lifetime of lane changes later, you arrive at a Red

Roof Inn in Natick. Cynthia, a tall, thin flute player from Boston, is inside, lying on one of the beds in your shared hotel room. She is already in her pajamas, watching TV and reading a book called *Get a Financial Life*.

"Sorry it's so late," you whisper, not bothering to introduce yourself. "It was a long trip, and then I had to help Becca unload and count the CDs."

Cynthia glances up from her book. "That's not in my job description," she says simply.

The next morning you reload the boxes of CDs into the rental car while Becca asks the hotel clerk for directions to the mall. Cynthia waits in her car, reading her book. But you don't mind lifting heavy boxes, even if it isn't in your "job description." You are too psyched to be on your way to your first official performance as a professional violinist, even though you know the audience won't hear a note you produce.

Because you grew up in the country, the American shopping mall was never a familiar place to you. Once or twice a year your mom would take you and your brothers to a mall in Northern Virginia. As a teenager, you looked forward to these trips—the malls in Fairfax and Tyson's Corner were full of novelties that weren't available to most teens in pre-Internet Appalachia: Doc Martens boots, t-shirts with alternative band logos, and endless accessories shops. But because these trips involved rushing from store to store, buying all the suburban goodies that your bumpkin family would need until next year's mall trip, you had never thought of a shopping mall as a place of casual leisure—the sort of place where people show up to take in the fountain scenery, eat junk food, and stroll around without shopping lists.

As you attempt to set up the concert apparatus, ensuring your violin will never be heard, you can't help but notice that the enclosed structure of a mall gives naked commerce a more sinister ambiance than the open-tent market of a craft fair. A craft fair is temporary— an occasion. At the New Hampshire craft fair you were the musical entertainment. But at the Massachusetts mall in Natick your performance competes with the music blaring out of each storefront, and the exhausted young shopkeepers glower out at you from their sunless corrals.

You begin to play but again struggle to follow the sheet music in front of you; you are still far from achieving the languid, semiconscious style of Yevgeny during an Ensemble performance. Cynthia, a professional flutist, confesses that she has never played the pennywhistle before and it might take her a while to get the hang of it. She squeaks and screeches. Becca reacts by turning up the volume on the CD music. Within minutes, a young mall security guard bellies up to Becca and tells her to turn it down—the shopkeepers in the nearby stores are complaining. Becca smiles sweetly and turns down the volume. As soon as his back is turned, she turns it back up.

A large group of customers gathers around the CD table and an outlying ring of shoppers listens from the second-floor balcony. They applaud after every song, gazing at you and Cynthia with looks of awe and respect. Between songs, customers ask you to autograph their CD purchases, and you do, never mentioning that you are not the violinist on the CDs. You bask in their admiration, relishing the thought that all of these strangers think you are amazingly talented. Meanwhile, Becca gives out CDs with one hand and takes cash with the other. The customers tell her, "It sounds like *Titanic*!" and ask her, "Who is The Composer?"

After an hour and four loops through the six-song set list, the security guard returns. He smiles at Becca apologetically, and she winks at him and laughs. You have to hand it to Becca—she is dedicated to the job. She turns down the volume and then turns it right back up again after the guard leaves.

The set list repeats and repeats. Cynthia squeaks. You miss your cues. It doesn't matter. Becca is selling boxes and boxes of CDs, and when twenty-dollar bills begin to overflow from the metal cash box, she starts throwing the cash into a large, cardboard CD box. Sometimes the customers shout, "Are they really playing?" and Becca nods her head yes. And it's true, you are really playing, though no one can hear a note over the blast of the speakers. You are beginning to relax and enjoy yourself, the way you used to enjoy hours of orchestra practice. The repetition of the music allows you to isolate certain violin skills and focus on improving them: bow hold, vibrato, dynamics, tone, and finger flexibility, a technique in which the right hand floats above the bow as if both are underwater. You are just beginning to experiment with a different finger positioning when something hits you on the head.

It is a penny. A group of Goth teenagers on the balcony is zinging pennies at you and Cynthia, as if you are the mall's wishing fountain. You are about to tell Becca that she has to make them stop when the mall guard walks up for the third time. He is now accompanied by a senior mall guard who begins yelling at Becca, loud enough that you can hear it over the relaxing sounds of *Titanic*: "You have to leave! You've been told three times you're too loud! We got complaints here! That's right—pack up!"

Becca's face turns fiery red. For a moment, you think senior mall guard is about to be gored on account of underestimating the bull. And you wonder if you and Cynthia—like the musicians on the RMS *Titanic*—should continue to play no matter what.

Instead, without warning, Becca cuts the power to the music.

You and Cynthia drop your instruments to your sides, instinctively maintaining the charade of "real" performance. And then, like an angry bull turned sweet, Becca turns to the crowd and yells: "They're kicking us out!"

You expect cheers—at least from the shopgirls and the penny-flinging Goths—but instead there is a chorus of boos.

"But it was beautiful! Beautiful music!" someone shouts.

"Let them stay! Let them stay!" others chant.

But the senior mall guard is adamant. No more music. Not today, not tomorrow, not ever. So you pack up the show and head back to New York. As she drives, Becca raps along to Eminem:

But no matter how many fish in the sea
It'll be so empty without me.

She pauses rapping only to take a call on her cell phone from Jake, The Composer's head manager. She explains the mall guard situation, and you are impressed; Becca makes it sound as if you and Cynthia are Shostakovich and Prokofiev, censored by Senior Mall Guard Joseph Stalin. But Jake doesn't seem bothered by your exile—your group has still made a considerable profit. He tells Becca to pay you for the entire weekend even though you only worked one day, and Becca hands you $450 in cash. As you head back to your dormitory, your hand keeps touching your pocket to make sure the bulge of twenties is still there.

Though it will take you years to recognize it, there was an additional form of currency in which you were being paid. The audience members at your concerts fell over themselves to adore you (sometimes literally, tripping as they moved trancelike toward the stage). Many of them wept as you played. Their constant stream of praise and adulation was as relentless as the music itself.

Many of the customers said they were "addicted" to The Composer's music, something you found ridiculous. What you didn't know at the time was that you were becoming addicted to the customers themselves, their endless praise for you, "such a talented violinist," "an amazing artist," someone with "a real gift."

God Bless America Tour 2004
Cartersville, Georgia

Our concerts in Orlando, Miami, and Tampa are canceled due to Hurricanes Charley, Ivan, and Frances. With our next concert five days away in Nashville, we decamp to a Hampton Inn on the outskirts of Cartersville, Georgia.

There is nothing to do and little to eat. We gather as much as we can from the free hotel breakfast each morning and order pizza each night from a place called "Pepperoni's," a name that suggests a living, breathing, walking stick of Pepperoni living in rural Georgia and running a pizza franchise. I go to the hotel gym each day to sweat on the elliptical while listening to Charlie Daniels on my iPod. I wonder how Charlie Daniels feels when he is on tour, all those people demanding the same songs over and over: "The Devil Went Down to Georgia," "The Orange Blossom Special." Over and over and over again. Year after year.

Charlie Daniels recorded a sequel to "The Devil Went Down to Georgia" called "The Devil Comes Back to Georgia." Johnny Cash sings it. I listen to it more times on the elliptical than I would want anyone to know about. The premise is simple: Ten years have passed since Johnny first beat the Devil in a fiddling contest. Now the Devil is back for a rematch. My favorite part of the song is when Johnny says he needs to go practice, and we get to hear him struggle to play the fiddle after ten years of not playing. He plays each note uncertainly, four times slower than normal. His hands have, in the words of the song, "grown cold." He practices more. His hands get warmer, faster. He goes double time, triple, until his fiddling is back up to its original, devil-beating speed. *The Devil's Dream is that he can win*, the song goes, *but Johnny is the best that's ever been*!

I used to think that the Devil versus Johnny was just a musical variation on the classic parable. The Devil attempting to steal a soul. Now, on the elliptical machine in rural Georgia, I wonder if it's more literal, if Charlie Daniels realized something in the years between the original Devil song and the sequel, something having to do with fans screaming requests for the same song night after night, year after year. The Devil coming back over and over again. The fear of having to beat him fresh each night.

Our hotel is surrounded by a forest. I stare at the empty parking lot through our bedroom window. The hurricane blows horizontal sheets of rain. We could move on to Nashville, where there is more to do and more to eat, but The Composer wants to stay in Cartersville where it is quiet, so he can finish his Christian musical. The musical is based on the Book of Ruth, an Old Testament story that begins with the search for food.

The Composer makes us a deal: If Harriet and I transcribe the violin parts for his musical, he will be able to finish early. If he can finish early, we will leave Cartersville and go somewhere more exciting.

"We can go to the Great Smokies," he says.

"How about Dollywood?" I ask. "It's only a few hours from here."

"Yes!" he shouts. "If we can finish this, we'll go to Dollywood!"

So Harriet and I set up musical transcription stations in our hotel room. We each have our own headphones, MP3 files sent to our email accounts, and sheets of music-composition paper. I listen to a track of chord progressions with vocals layered on top. I listen for the note most likely to be produced on a violin, the note that hovers on top of the sea of chords like a boat. Once I hear where the boat is, I plot its exact location. Using my violin, which I cradle in my lap and pluck, I identify the correct notes. I place these notes in their proper places on the staff-lined composition paper. I count beats with my foot, making sure that whole notes are whole, that three-quarter notes have a dot. It is challenging work. In a chord the notes blend together: A sounds like C, B sounds like D. I listen to the track over and over again, trying to banish from my head any lingering notes of "The Devil Went Down to Georgia" so as not to accidentally transcribe Johnny's fiddle music.

At some point I realize that the lyrics to The Composer's musical mention Jesus, even though the Book of Ruth is from the Old Testament. At some point I realize that The Composer has merely played some chords from his keyboard into a sophisticated computer recording system and emailed us an MP3. He has no idea how to write a violin part, which is why he's asked Harriet and me to do it. The pit violinists of this Christian musical I'm transcribing will never know that The Composer didn't fully write the music in front of them, couldn't have if he wanted to. They'll never know that the violin part was composed by a twenty-three-year-old amateur violinist working for free, and not for love of Jesus but for love of Dolly Parton. Whatever. I want to go to Dollywood. I want to eat something else besides stale bagels and slices of Supreme, which I order from Pepperoni's because it's the only way I can think of getting vegetables and protein.

But we never make it to Dollywood. We don't even go to the Great Smokies. We stay in Cartersville for five days, until the guys at Pepperoni's answer the phone and say, "Oh, hi, Jessica, a small Supreme?" Harriet and I complete days of free musical transcription for The Composer, a task that, had we been charging per hour, could have amounted to hundreds, possibly thousands of dollars. We complete free transcription for a musical about a woman who seeks food in a strange land and allows herself to be commandeered into a marriage to settle a property dispute. For this deed she's a commendable woman, worthy of her own musical. For this deed the man whom she is forced to marry says, "May you be blessed by the Lord, my daughter; this last instance of your loyalty is better than the first."

Who Is The Composer? II

What his fans say:

My wife and I met you at a craft show in Vermont. Since then we have played your music so much we are wearing the CDs thin. Your music helped us get through the death of our son. It has helped us survive and appreciate each moment. God Bless You!

Composer, I first stumbled on your music at a mall five years ago. I was entranced and moved to tears. Your CD *Oceans of April* has been with me through three surgeries to remove cancer. I am now in remission and am convinced that your music guided my recovery. I teach sixth graders and they beg me to play your music when they write in their journals. My greatest dream is for you to perform at the D—Junior High School, grades 6–8, so that you may bless our students through your music and they might find the health and peace that I have found through your stunning masterpieces.

Dear Composer,

I first heard your music on QVC. My son had just left for Iraq. I never thought I'd have a son go to war. It was the hardest time of my life. Our son lost many of his friends and my faith was tested every day, wondering if he would return. One day I heard your CDs on QVC and one song in particular left me in tears and strengthened my faith. In that instant I knew our son would come home safe and sound. Of course, I bought the six-CD set! Our son served another tour and was wounded, but he came home alive. Thank you for making music that touches the heart and reminds us we are all in God's hands.

Lincoln Center
New York City, 2002

A few days after your trip to the Massachusetts mall with Becca, she calls to ask if you can work the next weekend.

"The gig is at Lincoln Center," she says.

"Lincoln Center? Wait—*the* Lincoln Center?" you ask, thinking of the photo of The Composer conducting in Alice Tully Hall.

"Yeah. He will be the group leader."

"The Composer?"

"Yeah," she says. "Be at the fountain outside the main concert hall by 9 a.m. on Saturday."

The marble façades of Lincoln Center loom above you like alabaster temples, the arched windows of the Metropolitan Opera House revealing house-sized chandeliers. You are wearing new clothes and shoes that you have bought with the express purpose of tricking The Composer into thinking you are a polished professional: a cream-colored flowered top, brown wool skirt lined with red silk, and brown wedge heels that sting the backs of your ankles with their unbroken leather. You have curled the wild ends of your hair into a neat bob. As you ascend the gleaming white stairs that separate the Lincoln Center campus from the street, violin case strapped to your back, you notice that rows of canopy tents have been erected all over the main plaza. The tents are full of merchandise: handmade journals, South American blankets, wooden figurines of African animals, Thai food, corn on the cob. *There must be some sort of street fair going on*, you think. Then, just as you reach the fountain—the glittering aquatic architecture anchoring one of the world's largest venues for the high arts—you hear the unmistakable siren of a pennywhistle. It dawns on you that you will not be performing in the five-tiered auditorium with velvet seats and diamond chandeliers, but outside on the sun-bleached concrete. Who could have guessed Lincoln Center doubles as a craft fair campground?

You follow the sound of the pennywhistle to a white tent situated between the Koch ballet theater and the Metropolitan Opera House. The Composer sits on a folding chair arranging his CDs on the sales table. You recognize him immediately from the photo on his CD cover, taken just a few dozen feet away inside the grand Alice Tully concert hall, where he conducted one of our nation's most elite orchestras. In person, you realize he is even more youthful and handsome than his CD cover suggests. He is thin with a generous scoop of dark hair, large brown doe-eyes, high cheekbones, and a square jaw.

"HELLO, SIR!" you yell over the music. "I'M JESSICA HIND-MAN, THE VIOLINIST." The Composer looks up at you with a dazed expression. He gestures for you to come back behind the speakers.

"Thanks for coming," he says in a voice so soft you have to lean toward him to hear it. "It's cool you made it. We're going to have a lot of fun today. It's going to be awesome."

You nod enthusiastically. Cool. Fun. Awesome.

You notice the flute player standing in the back of the tent, a petite woman in her early thirties with wispy strawberry-blond hair and small blue eyes. The Composer returns to his seat without introducing you to her, and you wait for her to say something first. You unpack your violin and rosin your bow. Finally, you smile shyly and introduce yourself.

"Kim," she says in response, looking away. She leaves her post behind the microphones and walks behind The Composer, whispering something in his ear while glancing back at you. You shift on your feet, pretending to examine every millimeter of your violin. Have you done something wrong? Can they tell your violin is cheap? That you are really just a poor college student masquerading as a professional musician?

"Do you know the songs?" The Composer asks.

"Yes!" you say, hoping to win him over with the brute force of your enthusiasm. "I've practiced and I'm close to having everything memorized."

"So . . . um . . . you know, when the music starts, you keep playing . . . no matter what."

"Of course," you say, smiling your biggest, most compliant grin. "I understand how it works."

You start the set list. Kim plays her part flawlessly, sending the notes of the almost-*Titanic* soundtrack sailing high into the air over Lincoln Center. She is actually the flutist who performs on the CDs, so her instrument and playing style in the tent is a perfect match with the recording coming from the speakers.

Even though you know no one in the audience can hear you, you want to make sure The Composer knows you can play his music. Whenever the music calls for a note to be emphasized, you play it with dramatic vibrato that gives the notes a bold, pulsing tone. You sway with the watery crescendos in "Ocean's Cliff," and you use your entire bow for the violin solos in "Birds of Moonrise," making dramatic lifts and sweeps with each passage.

Two hours later, you take a ten-minute break. The Composer walks over to speak to you. There is something about his demeanor that reminds you of a kitten. He has a frightened yet confident look in his darting eyes.

"Hey . . . um," he says. "Melissa?"

"Jessica," you say.

"Yeah. You're doing a really great job. Really great," he almost whispers, staring above your head. "Really nice . . . but . . . um . . . it's really important to remember to play very quietly. Can you play very quietly?"

"Yes," you say, your voice coming out as barely a whisper.

You put a small black rubber mute on the bridge of your violin and spend the next two hours playing so softly that you can't even hear yourself. You play all of the notes with your fingers but use only a single bow hair, producing an almost inaudible puff of sound. When you take your next break, The Composer tells you that you have done "a really awesome job."

"The only thing is," he says, "could you smile a bit more?"

"Okay," you say. Then you realize you aren't smiling when you say it. So you smile (you've already learned to do so on command from years of *life in the body*) and The Composer smiles back.

And you begin another two-hour set.

The afternoon sun beats down and the temperature inside the tent creeps upward. Your wool skirt—which seemed sensible in the cool hours of the September morning—becomes sweaty and itchy around the waistband. As you enter your sixth hour playing along with the CD, you begin to struggle. In high school you occasionally attended eight-hour practice sessions for regional orchestra events, but those rehearsals always involved sitting on stage in an air-conditioned auditorium with frequent breaks while the conductor focused on different sections of the orchestra. You have never played like this—nonstop, for hours, in heat, like a musical automaton. Sweat trickles down your spine, your throat becomes parched, and a bagel you wolfed down during the break churns like wet cement in your stomach. You shift your weight from foot to foot as your new shoes cut bloody blisters into your heels. You curse yourself for playing so exuberantly in the first hours of the gig. One by one your muscles begin to protest: first your shoulders, then your back. By hour six, flames of pain engulf your chin, neck, arms, wrists, and hands until even the wisps of nerve endings in your fingertips are ablaze. By the eighth hour, you stoop in front of your microphone like an elderly woman, barely able to move your arms.

To take your mind off your increasing pain and exhaustion, you study The Composer's interactions with the customers. Unlike the ones in New Hampshire and Massachusetts, almost none of the New York City customers have heard of The Composer or his music. They stride up to the CD table in their weekend loafers, gumming the lids of their Starbucks cups.

It sounds like Titanic, they say.

The Composer nods.

Who is The Composer?

"I am," he says.

That is all the information they need. They don't ask what song is playing now, or remark that the music is beautiful or relaxing. They don't justify their purchases to everyone around them by proclaiming that they *need* relaxing CDs because they are divorced, or work with children, or have diabetes. You wait for someone to say that listening to a *Titanic* knockoff soundtrack will be an ironic guilty pleasure, enjoyed between finer pastimes such as going to gallery openings and reading the *New Yorker*, but no one does. Instead, they take out their leather billfolds, snap out crisp one-hundred-dollar bills, tell The Composer they'd like one of each of the nine CDs, nod to you and Kim, and leave as quickly as they came. One man leaves two twenty-dollar bills for you and Kim as a tip. And it occurs to you that the only major difference between The Composer's customers in rural America and his customers in Manhattan—the epicenter of elite musical culture—is the amount of money they can spend on CDs, and the speed at which they part with their cash.

At 6 p.m. The Composer cuts the power to the music. You peel your violin from your neck. The rosewood endpin has cut into the soft flesh above your carotid artery, leaving a large hickey-like sore. The fingertips on your left hand are grooved in the shape of strings, and the thumb on your right hand has been deformed by eight hours of pressing into the frog of the bow; it is now a half thumb. When The Composer hands you your money—$150 for eight hours of playing plus the customer's $20 tip—your hand wavers under the bills with a Parkinsonian tremble.

Let Us Now Speak of The Money

L et us now speak of The Money that The Composer put into your trembling hand, your need for it, your relationship to it. Let us say that your need to make tuition money—lots of it, fast—made you different from your classmates, many of whom had attended prestigious boarding schools where tuition matched or even exceeded Columbia's. Let us say that being different at Columbia, like any place, led to a certain isolation, and that this isolation was sometimes self-imposed, a way to protect yourself against the rage stalking the periphery of your consciousness. Let us acknowledge that as a doctor's daughter, your family was upper-middle class by the time you graduated from high school, and that to be upper-middle class in Appalachia is to be rich. Let us also acknowledge that groveling for tuition money because one's parents have never heard of Columbia and refuse to pay its exorbitant tuition is, within the Ivy League, to be poor. Let us confess that to be rich in one world and poor in another is a confusing situation for an eighteen-year-old to find herself in.

Let us add that a mind-boggling number of Columbia students hailed from a socioeconomic class you'd never come into contact with before: the richest of the rich. Several of the parents who moved their kids into your freshman dormitory were household-name celebrities. Let us speak of private planes, of multiple mansions, of oil investments, of foreign royalty. Of Congress and the White House and Wall Street and Hollywood and the personal connections to all of these represented by your classmates. Let us now speak of The Money, a subject that always feels like it needs permission to be discussed aloud, a treacherous minefield in which you operated as a double agent. Let us now speak of The Money, a subject even more taboo at Columbia than rape.

Let us emphasize that, surprisingly, your biggest problem with The Money did not stem from your need for more of it. Yes, there were moments when you were blindsided with feelings of self-pity, moments when you wept in the damp, empty laundry rooms of dormitories during spring break, all of your friends having departed for Paris or Tahoe or New Orleans or St. Maarten. But these moments were rare. You did not mind having to make money for tuition, even via ridiculous and unhealthy schemes like egg donation, nor did you bemoan your inability to spend money as freely as your classmates. Let us confess that your struggles for The Money became a point of pride, one of the few points of pride you could locate on the map of your general mediocrity.

Let us now emphasize that your real problem with The Money was a cultural, geographical problem, sown deep in the soil of your mountain-shadowed childhood. Your problem with The Money was the fact that its very existence went ignored at Columbia. Your problem with The Money was that it was a subject that intrigued and embarrassed your classmates (and some of your professors) in a way that made you suspect they had never considered The Money before.

Let us say that it bothered you, a doctor's daughter, to be the only emissary of the Appalachian poor to the coastal rich. Let us say that the kids in your high school—the ones who dropped out to work nights at the chicken plant, the ones who were snatched up by the tables of Army recruiters in your high school's main corridor, the ones who disappeared into pregnancy, vocational school, alcohol, or drugs—would probably never have chosen you to be their voice, but that you spoke for them anyway because it enraged you when Columbia students attributed their life successes to hard work and talent, when plenty of hardworking, talented folks you knew were spending their days serving chicken-fried steaks and scrubbing floors and sweating through basic training. Let us confess that you were better able to see these injustices now that you were, for the first time in your life, the person whom others thought of as poor.

Let us now speak of the children of the American suburbs, a group with its own culture and subcultures, a species as foreign to you as wild chimpanzees, their hometown neighborhoods so stratified and gated and segregated that the kids who lived in million-dollar houses rarely mingled with the kids who lived in $800,000 houses. As someone who had grown up in towns that were their own contained worlds—not satellite neighborhoods orbiting massive cities—such minute segregation by income was a new concept. Let us say that the thing you most wanted to articulate to your classmates was information about a world outside suburban and urban wealth, a world beyond elite boarding schools (the names of which you were beginning to learn in order to navigate the large groups of people at Columbia who already knew one another from high school), a world in which most people don't go to college at all— which is not, not, *not* the same thing as being lazy or stupid. Let us say that people in Appalachia are no smarter or dumber than people from other places. Even as you tried to impart this information, you failed miserably. What you ended up imparting, more often than not, was this: The Appalachian South equals funny accents, pickup trucks, racists, venison dinners, buttermilk biscuits, sweet tea. Let us acknowledge your failure to do justice to the wonderful and miserable complexities of the culture in which you were raised, and let us hypothesize that many people who you grew up with would have done a better job of it.

But let us also say that your admission to Columbia—very likely a result of your geographical and cultural identity, one you were savvy enough at seventeen to play up in a college admissions essay full of dairy cows and country music—came without any allowance for the fact that to admit a token Appalachian kid is also to be responsible for her acclimation to a world in which she is culturally and financially foreign. Let us suggest that you had been set up by a system to confirm the Northeastern elite's preexisting biases about the rural South.

Let us acknowledge that out of the nine hundred students in your year, at least a few had to be poor (and not just Columbia-poor, like you, but poor-poor). Perhaps a few were also from Appalachia. Even as these students must have existed, you rarely met one of them, possibly because you were all working so much you didn't have time to find each other at social events. Or perhaps you did meet but never identified yourselves, too embarrassed or exhausted to bring up the taboo subject of The Money. Let us acknowledge that just outside the campus gates, on the streets of upper Manhattan, were plenty of people who were definitively poor, who lived in a poverty that was far deeper and more complex than having no tuition money. One homeless man screamed nonstop for hours outside your dormitory window each night. Those screams sounded primal and terrifying. Let us confess that you learned to ignore these screams, could even, by the end of your sophomore year, sleep through them.

Let us explain that the Ensemble gigs—which you started working every weekend and almost always involved long journeys by car or plane—began on Thursday nights and ended on Sunday evenings: a seventy-two-hour work cycle with no time to study or write papers. Let us acknowledge that during the week you worked additional jobs. Let us confess that you struggled with addiction, that what began with coffee and then cigarettes accelerated into Adderall and cocaine, and that you used these stimulants to stay awake Monday through Thursday in order to work and study. You intended to graduate a year early to save money; because of this you signed up for heavy course loads. Let us acknowledge that stimulant abuse cut into The Money that you were staying awake to earn.

Let us acknowledge that after you exhausted the scholarships, the money from egg donation, the jobs, and the maximum amount of student loans one can take out, your upper-middle-class parents ended up paying ("loaning" was the word they used) the remaining tuition. Let us state for the record that by the time your parents did this it was too late; something deep within you had changed. Perhaps it happened during the Air Force ROTC drills, or the night with Rose in Penn Station, or at the egg donation clinic. Perhaps it happened after the seventh hour of an eight-hour stretch playing the violin like a robot. Perhaps it happened when you realized you had stayed awake too many days working and studying, that your neurological and cardiovascular systems were mortal, that your body was begging you to lay off the stimulants to go to sleep. Whatever the cause, it happened: something inside of you broke down, disintegrated, evaporated. Poof. Something inside of you shed its soft skin and became tough. Too tough.

Let us quote Virginia Woolf, who famously wrote about her days of needing The Money: "I need not, I am afraid, describe in any detail the hardness of the work, for you know perhaps women who have done it; nor the difficulty of living on the money when it was earned, for you may have tried. But what still remains with me as a worse infliction than either was the poison of fear and bitterness those days bred in me."

And let us confess that for a few years you blamed your parents, and then yourself, for this too-tough thing inside of you, this fear and bitterness, when in truth it was not your parents' fault, nor yours. In your own ways, you and your parents were equally clueless about The Money, vulnerable to its complexities and confusions and emotions, all of you facing a two thousand-foot mountain barrier to accessing another, unknown world. Let us say that there was little to guide you but love, luck, and violin music.

God Bless America Tour 2004
Nashville

The Composer tells us, "There are people out there dying of cancer, guys," and though Harriet and I make fun of him for it when he's not around, he has a point. A disproportionate number of our audience members are elderly or ill or survivors of life's grimmest ordeals. After each concert, The Composer listens to each and every person. If there are four hundred audience members and it takes three hours, he will listen to them until the last person has left. Sometimes the stragglers follow him back to the RV, as if they are hoping we will take them with us on tour. They tell The Composer that they have gone through cancer, that their son was killed in a car accident, that their husband was in the hospital for months after his last heart attack. They tell The Composer that his music is what helped them go on. Sometimes they claim his music cured them of cancer, diabetes, high blood pressure. The Composer calls these fans "hardcore."

Sometimes these hardcore fans are kids. The Composer talks to each one and asks them if they play an instrument. If they do, he tells them to keep at it. To practice. To watch PBS specials of great performances. To do well in school. The kids do what I remember doing when adults spoke to me like this: They act shy, but they are listening.

Unlike the craft fair and mall gigs where customers sometimes ask, "Are they really playing?" no one in any of our PBS concert audiences ever questions the authenticity of our performance. The idea of sitting through an hour-long "concert" that is mostly a CD recording is likely too embarrassing to even contemplate, let alone ask one of us about.

One night I overhear The Composer speaking with a tearful woman who has waited for an hour after the concert to speak to him. Her son has been deployed to Iraq since the war began, she tells him.

The Composer sits with her for a long time, listening and nodding. The woman's son is being transferred tomorrow to be a medic in the Special Forces. It's a more dangerous assignment.

"I will pray he returns safely," The Composer says in a soft but genuine voice of concern. It is clear that the woman is comforted by his presence. She brushes her dark hair away from her eyes, which are no longer full of tears.

"I want him back here now," she says. "But he says he doesn't want to come home until the job is done."

"That must be so hard for you."

"Listening to your music really helps," she says. "It is so calming. It gives me a few minutes of peace. You played so beautifully up on that stage. I really loved it. I really needed a night like this."

"Thank you," he says. "God bless you." And then, without any awkwardness, he wraps his arms around her and gives her a long hug.

Itzhak Perlman Leaves the Concert Early
New York City, 2000

One of the first of many jobs you work in New York City is as an assistant for a production company that organizes major concert events for Carnegie Hall, including "Fiddle Fest," the charity concert for a Harlem string program featured in the 1999 Meryl Streep movie *Music of the Heart*. The Harlem kids are still fiddling their hearts out onstage when your boss asks you to find Itzhak Perlman in his dressing room and ask him if he will be performing what she calls "the Palladio." Perlman has already performed several pieces that night and the producers have made the Palladio optional for him.

Regardless of whether Itzhak Perlman participates in it or not, the Palladio is sure to be a crowd-pleaser. It is a piece that has been chosen for this concert not for its complexity or rich musical history but because it was featured in the 1990s De Beers diamond commercials, the ones where husband-and-wife silhouettes progress through life's touching milestones—the husband carrying his new bride over the threshold to their kid's college graduation. Audiences love the Palladio; it is simple, dramatic, and comes with a preexisting set of mental images.

When you were in high school, teachers and other students would occasionally ask you to play the Palladio (though everyone, yourself included, knew it only as "the diamond commercial song"). It was up there with "the beef commercial song" (Copland's Hoedown), "that Mozart song" (Eine Kleine Nachtmusik), and "The Devil Went Down to Georgia" on every violinist's list of Most Clichéd Requests.

And now you are going to go ask Itzhak Perlman, the most famous violinist in the world, if he will play it.

You are very nervous.

You knock softly on the open door of his dressing room.

There he is, Itzhak Perlman, looking older than the photographs on your CD jackets. He is seated at one of those vanity tables that have lightbulbs around the mirror.

"Excuse me, Mr. Perlman," you half-whisper. "They need to know if you will be performing the Palladio."

The famous, legendary Perlman—looking at you! *Listening* to you!

"It's pronounced Pa-LAH-dio," he says, annoyed. "And no, I'm going home."

Cairo, Egypt

2001

B y the end of your freshman year of college, you have dropped any lingering pretentions of majoring in music or becoming a professional musician. The scariest part about giving up the dream to become a violinist is the absence of a dream large enough to take its place. But gradually, and then quite dramatically, something else does.

It begins, like so many interests that begin in college, when you are assigned a random course on a subject you know nothing about: Introduction to Islamic Civilization. You have no idea what Islam is, let alone Islamic civilization, but as you slog through the assigned readings and the discussion sections, you begin to realize that this is a field of study where your ignorance might be an advantage. While your classmates fight the Israeli-Palestinian conflict in each seminar, boys wearing yarmulkes trading heated jibes with girls in hijabs, you observe silently from the back of the classroom. Before going to college, you had never met a Muslim or Arab, and the only Jewish person you had ever known was your ex-boyfriend Fernando, whose family was half Jewish, religiously unobservant, and politically ambiguous. While a surprising number of your Muslim and Jewish classmates struggle with the urge to write one-sided political polemics, you are able, by no other virtue than being unfamiliar and unaffiliated with either side, to take a more objective approach. You begin to realize that you are receiving the top grades in these courses—that your rural-bred ignorance, in this one discipline, gives you an undeserved but real edge. You don't spend much time worrying about the absurd irony that your lack of knowledge about the Middle East is what's helping you excel in Middle Eastern studies. You just enroll in more courses: Zionism, The Quran, Palestinian Literature, The Egyptian Novel, Arab and Israeli Women's Literature. By the end of your sophomore year, the spring of 2001, your major is Middle Eastern studies, you are capable of writing twenty-page papers about the destruction of religious icons in Taliban-run Afghanistan, and you have decided to study abroad in Cairo in the fall so that you can learn Arabic.

You leave for Cairo on August 19, 2001. The first few weeks of your study abroad experience are spent learning the new currency, the essential Arabic phrases needed to buy groceries or ask for directions, the layout of Cairo, and how to live as a woman in a city that is recognized as the world capital of street harassment.

Then one afternoon, around 4 p.m. Cairo time, just a few weeks into the semester, you stroll into the smoky student cafeteria after Arabic class to get a snack, shooing a stray cat off a chair so you can sit. You notice a TV across the room with a crowd of people around it. It is showing Al Jazeera streaming CNN, which is depicting live footage of two blazing holes in the World Trade Center towers. It immediately becomes apparent that your study abroad experience in the Middle East is going to be very different from the one you had been expecting.

The first order of business is to ascertain whether or not the United States is about to bomb the living shit out of Egypt, the home country of head-hijacker Mohammad Atta, whose family home is a few blocks away from the cat-filled student cafeteria. It takes a few days before that scenario is seen to be unlikely. There is a mandatory meeting at the American Embassy for all Americans in Cairo. The ambassador explains the evacuation procedures. Many Americans—including the majority in your study abroad program—flee to Europe (it will be weeks before international flights are allowed into the United States). But you do not want to go. You see now that this study abroad experience could be a direct pipeline to a future career. The United States will need people like you, people who know about the Middle East. So you stay in Cairo, along with a few dozen other American students.

Your classes are canceled for a week while the Egyptian military surrounds the campus with soldiers and tanks. You leave the student hostel, which seems like it could be a target, to join six other American students in a penthouse apartment near Tahrir Square. For days after the attacks, the six of you watch Al Jazeera, drink Nescafé, and chain-smoke Cleopatra cigarettes. When you tire of watching gruesome footage on TV, you climb to the roof of the apartment building and look out across the rooftops of Cairo as the muezzin calls the evening prayer. In the coming months, you and the other students experience an aftermath of September 11th that is radically unlike the American one. You navigate the complexities of the Cairene streets, where some Egyptians personally apologize for the attacks, while others claim that the United States or Israel have staged the attacks as an excuse to kill Muslims. You and the other students find yourselves in strange political waters, defending George W. Bush to Egyptians who suddenly think he is Hitler, blasting him over email to Americans back home who suddenly think he is Jesus.

As you stand on a Cairo rooftop while thousands of muezzin sing "Allāhu Akbar," you come to understand that your violin—which you have left behind in the States—will be truly abandoned in the pursuit of another dream: to become a journalist in the Middle East. What you're really thinking is war correspondent, and in preparation for your future résumé, you begin to write articles about what you witness in Cairo and email them to your hometown newspaper, which publishes them verbatim. Becoming a war correspondent seems like an easily achievable goal, for it looks certain that there will be a war, the kind of war people your age know about only from grandparents and history books. It is hard at first for you and the other American students in Cairo to articulate what you are feeling, but you try, in the only language that seems appropriate: the language of Hollywood. You actually say to one another, "The whole world is on fire," as if you are the lovers in *The Last of the Mohicans*, the movie's famous violin soundtrack looping in the background of the blaze. You know this is the apocalypse because you've seen it before in *Independence Day* and *Deep Impact* and *Armageddon* and *Fight Club*. It is almost as if, in planning the attacks, the terrorists have used your own movies against you.

And yet here you are, this tiny circle of Americans, college juniors who have already spent years at university studying the Middle East, students who are so dedicated that you aren't fleeing the region like the other Americans. You argue about culture and language and religion and politics, but on one thing you are in agreement: You have all chosen your majors wisely. You will all be able to help with this crisis, this scary new reality. Your once-obscure studies of Arab language, literature, culture, and religion will surely now be acknowledged by everyone back home as useful and relevant and well chosen. You can prevent more bloodshed. You can build understanding. You will be put to good use by news organizations or think tanks or the State Department. You are all the heroes of this movie, for the heroes of such movies are always the nerds, the professors, the ones who speak the language, the ones who have the crucial info, the intel, the scoop.

There is no way of knowing that ten years after you stand on that rooftop, watching the sun set over Cairo, the last one of your group will slouch homeward, feeling defeated after years of struggling to make a living as a foreign correspondent, despite his fluency in Arabic and talent for analyzing complex and dangerous situations in Iraq and Lebanon and Libya. There is no way to know that the new America will have very little interest in learning anything accurate about the Middle East—that instead there are powerful interests that will need Americans to think of the Middle East as a homogeneous region full of terrorists. That Afghanistan and Saudi Arabia and Iraq and Iran are all the same. An acidic current of anti-intellectualism and prowar sentiment will corrode nuance, subtlety, and complexity into a dull, generalized fear. As you stand on the roof in Cairo with six other young, idealistic Americans on the dawn of a new era, you have no idea that despite hailing from the best Middle Eastern studies programs in the country at Georgetown and Yale and Columbia, despite studying abroad in the Middle East during a time of crisis, despite learning Arabic and analyzing the Quran and spending months assimilating into Arab culture—it will be more difficult to make a living by providing accurate information about the Middle East to an American audience than it will be to make a living by fake-playing the violin.

Kansas

September 2002

A few days after the gig at the Lincoln Center craft fair, Becca Belge calls again.

"Can you work this weekend?" she asks.

"Of course."

"Great. You're going to Kansas."

"Kansas?"

"Yep. Motherfucking Kansas!"

You have never been somewhere so full of endless yellow light. In the early morning the fields outside of Wichita blaze for miles. Sunflowers, rows and rows of them, each one a tiny fire burning through the morning mist. You watch the sunflowers and the weather vanes and the grain silos pass by from the backseat of a rented minivan. The Composer is driving, Kim sits beside him. Neither one speaks to you.

You arrive at a large fairground and set up the equipment on the stage of an outdoor amphitheater. The Composer and Kim stick together while you set up your music stand and rosin your bow in silence. Just as with the other venues, crowds of customers mob the CD table as soon as you and Kim begin to play. They *ooh* and *ahh* at the sounds of *Titanic* but are more discerning in their purchases than the Lincoln Center crowd, spending time weighing their options, selecting only one or two CDs. An outer ring of audience members forms around the customers. They watch you for hours; some even go to their cars and return with lawn seats and picnic blankets. Their spouses or adult children join them with refreshments—whole turkey legs, country ham sandwiches, cotton candy—and they listen as you loop and loop through the set list, not realizing or not caring that they are listening to the same six three-minute songs over and over again.

From your post behind the microphone, you study the Kansans. The men wear FDNY baseball caps with etchings of the Twin Towers; the women wear t-shirts with the words "We Will Never Forget." Though it has only been a year since the attacks, you rarely see such patriotic attire on New Yorkers, at least not on the Upper West Side. Most of the New Yorkers you know are struggling to achieve what the Kansans' t-shirts warn against: forgetfulness. New Yorkers know the danger of remembering too much. Their memories might make it impossible to go to work every day on the subway, to take an elevator, to leave one's warm bed in the morning.

"You must be so scared," a Kansas woman says as you man the CD table while The Composer and Kim get lunch.

"Not really," you say.

"My wife and I are saving to go there," another Kansan says. He is wearing an FDNY t-shirt and a somber expression. "To see Ground Zero. I've never been out East. But we want to go now and pay our respects."

You notice that The Composer's music—which is blasting out of the speakers at its usual rib cage–rattling volume—imbues these conversations with a heightened sense of importance, enhances the depth of the tragedy. It seems impossible, but with The Composer's music playing in the background, September 11th becomes even more dramatic.

"You play such beautiful music," says one elderly woman. "We need music like this in times like these."

The Geography of a Lead-Up to a War

OCTOBER 2002

"I have a suspicion," the professor says. He is older, maybe in his seventies, with white tufts of hair sprouting from his ears and nostrils. He emigrated from the Middle East at a young age, studied in Europe, and now speaks with a faint German accent. He is brilliant and lively and you love him and his course, Theories of Middle Eastern Culture.

"All of you are upperclassmen, correct?" he asks.

Correct.

"All of you are Middle Eastern studies majors, correct?"

We are.

"And it is true this so-called Middle Eastern studies department is seen to be the best of its kind in the country? Perhaps the world?"

It is.

"Excellent, excellent, very good," he says. "And you can all argue the theoretical points and counterpoints, perform Foucaultian analysis on Egyptian novels, delineate the important post-colonial theories and their relationship to Palestinian poetry, apply feminist theory to Quranic verse. I have seen you do so. Very well."

"But," he continues, "if I pass out a map of the Middle East right now, a blank map, can you fill in the names of each country?"

We look around nervously.

"I have this *suspicion*—it is small but *very* insistent—that perhaps you are not able to do this thing," he says. "You are all very smart. Yes, very smart. But do you know the precise location of things?"

"I know where Jordan is," your friend Ahmed calls out from the back of the room. We laugh. Ahmed's uncle is King Hussein of Jordan.

"Very well!" the professor says. "But what about the rest of you? Can you locate Jordan? Do you know Iran from Iraq? How to be sure? Ah! A quiz!"

He passes out photocopies of a blank map of the Middle East and tells us we have ten minutes to show him our knowledge of geography. He says, "Let us see how many of you—the so-called best and brightest Americans—know the precise location of the country you are about to invade."

NOVEMBER 2002

"Where is the main courtyard?" you ask the mall security guard. You are somewhere in Connecticut, though you aren't sure which part or which city. Not that it matters, as malls in Connecticut tend to be the same: large and fancy and full of people buying Christmas presents, weeks before the Thanksgiving bird has been cooked.

After your gig with The Composer in Kansas, you begin to go on gigs every weekend. Every Thursday night you meet someone from the Ensemble—sometimes Yevgeny, sometimes Becca, sometimes a musician you have never met before and will never see again. They pick you up outside of your dormitory or meet you at an airport or train station or bus depot. You take night buses to Buffalo and Albany and Vermont. Flights to Oklahoma City and Fayetteville, Arkansas. You wake up on Friday mornings and ask, "Where the . . .?" and the answer is Miami. Or Cleveland. Or Washington, D.C. You learn to open up the drawer next to the hotel bed, the one with the Bible in it, and look for the phone book, which will reveal where you are: Scranton, Pennsylvania; Ocean City, Maryland; Providence, Rhode Island; Rochester, New York. You return, exhausted, to your dorm on Sunday nights with jugs of craft fair apple cider and write papers about the ongoing feud between Edward Said and Bernard Lewis. Bernard Lewis claims that all Arabs have a hidden terrorist bone. Edward Said offers, as counterevidence, the fact that he loves classical music and is proficient at the piano. If you are going to tackle this level of bullshit on no sleep, you're going to need something stronger than coffee. A friend swears cocaine has miraculous effects on the quality of her essay assignments. She offers you a half gram. You snort line after line and stay up for three days writing a paper in which you call both Said and Lewis ridiculous, elitist old men. Men who have no idea what life is like for real Americans (read: West Virginians), or real Arabs (read: the few poor Egyptians you had conversations with in Cairo), or women (read: you). You get an A on this paper. You write more, you get more As. You learn to write while shaking, how to go to class on no sleep. You lose weight—weight you don't need to lose—and you look skeletal, anemic, ill, yet people compliment your weight loss, another paradox of *life in the body*. You receive a letter from your mom. She is worried you might be on drugs. You assure her you are not—not so much because you are ashamed to tell her that you are on drugs (though you are ashamed) but because you are ashamed to tell her that some of the money you make each week ($50 of the $450) is being spent on them. You convince yourself that she will not understand this complicated calculus of drugs and money—the whole point of using drugs is so you can make money in the first place—and write back to tell her everything is fine.

A few days later the professor with the white hair tufting out of his ears and nose passes back the map quizzes. As he suspected, many of the best and brightest Americans have failed, do not know the precise location of the country we are about to invade. But your map has an A on it, even though you forgot the existence of Qatar and Bahrain. You have never done this well in school. You have never made this much money. You have never received so many compliments on your appearance, for your body is shrinking into a landless skeletal border, and a landless skeletal border is your nation's preferred female shape. You have never been so close to killing yourself, not with drugs, which are merely a symptom, but with overwork— your real disease. It's a disease you were born with, fertilized with mountain fog—the desire to flee small-town Appalachia, the guilt

of doing so, the suspicion that you are, at your core, a fraud. The
only cure is to work more. Work harder than anyone else.

"Where is the main courtyard?" you ask another mall guard, this
time in Maryland.

"It's in front of the Abercrombie, which is next to the yogurt
place, which is near the Macy's," he replies. A geography of commerce that you navigate like a seasoned sea captain in port. You lead
the other musicians to the courtyard, for you are now a leader of
fake musicians, the one who knows how to set up and break down
the sound equipment, the one who knows how to count the CDs
and the money. The one who knows the exact location at which the
speakers must be angled to draw in the maximum amount of customers, the precise geography of sound, the point on the map where
the human ear can no longer distinguish real sound from fake.

DECEMBER 2002

"West Virginia!" the therapist at Psychological Services exclaims.
"You are a real country girl! You actually grew up there? Like
with cows?"

You have made an appointment in an attempt to confess your
troubles, specifically your drug abuse, to someone, anyone. But you
want to ease into it. You don't want to be mistaken for someone
you're not (party girl!). But before you can tell her anything, about
the drugs or the need for tuition money, the isolation or the feelings
of failure in the midst of seeming success, she becomes distracted
by geography.

"West Virginia!"

She is a native New Yorker, upper class, most likely the grand-
daughter of immigrants—though whether Italian or Jewish or some

other extraction you cannot tell, and it doesn't matter, because the main ethnicity, the defining characteristic, is native New Yorker. Perhaps your ancestors were on the same boat as hers, but upon reaching Ellis Island they disembarked to different planets—hers to a factory on the Lower East Side, yours to the West Virginia mines. Now, decades later, their descendants struggle to comprehend one another. You have learned to spot and identify them, the native New Yorkers, by their accents, their words trumpeting out of their nasal cavities, their sentences a brassy scale. It's also her shoes, which you would have once thought of as plain, but which you can now identify as expensive.

"West Virginia!" she exclaims again, shaking her head in amazement. And you love her for thinking this is interesting. You love her even more for thinking this makes *you* interesting, a standout among her usual patients. But you also realize she's not going to be able to help you.

Yes, you say. And you spend the rest of your time describing the landscape, the geography of mountains and luck, the border between West Virginia and western Virginia that determined your destiny, the mountain shadows and the sun-spackled valleys. And the cows.

A few days later you find yourself shaking in bed at dawn, coked-up to the rafters. Despite not sleeping for the past two nights, you are awake. Too awake. Terrified. You haven't told a soul that you are afraid you're on the verge of a heart attack or stroke or whatever bad fate happens to young stupid college girls from the country (cows!). But now you call the person in your life who you trust the most, who you have spent the most time with over the past six months, on long car rides and at fast-food restaurants and watching bad hotel TV. A person who fixes problems better and faster than anyone you have ever met, from a lost hotel reservation to a flat tire to a broken violin string. A person who navigates America the way that only a foreigner can, with an eye to its nuances, its foot-scented stickers, its strange music, its abundance of pocket money for relaxing CDs. A person who, even though he never went to college and just learned to speak English a few years ago, seems infinitely more capable of helping you than anyone at school.

He comes right away, looking miserable as ever in the dull light of midmorning, and sits beside you while you lie in bed. His eyes are gray and hard and rimmed with circles, his white-blond hair slicked back, giving him the look of an eagle. He puts a hand on your head and promises to stay to make sure you keep breathing. And when you wake up, a few hours later, feeling a world better, he is still there, and he tells you a story.

"Did I ever tell you what I did before I worked for The Composer?" Yevgeny asks.

"Yes, you worked at a butcher shop. You almost sliced off your fingers," you say.

"No, before that. When I was *really* desperate," he says.

"No, tell me."

His job, the first he took when he came to America seeking a better life, speaking no English, and having no money, was to put stickers advertising a towing company on pay phones in Manhattan. Every day he would return to the same phones and his stickers would be gone, replaced by the stickers of rival towing companies. He'd peel those stickers off and put his stickers on, and then the next day they would be gone again. Day after day. Month after month. In the rain, the snow, the heat.

Until one day he couldn't take it anymore. There were just some things you couldn't do for money. Not because they were particularly difficult, but because you just didn't want to. Because they weren't worth your life, which might not be worth much, but was worth something.

After the day with Yevgeny, you quit using drugs. Years later, the simplicity of this—you quit using drugs—strikes you as miraculous. A bit too miraculous. It makes you doubt the seriousness of your drug abuse, which, after all, lasted only a few months. What seems most important is that, for the first time in your life, you chose your health over the extra work that you might have been able to produce, the extra success you might have been able to achieve, had you kept doing drugs for a few more months or years until you collapsed. You'll feel incredibly lucky that, when it came to quitting drugs, things were so easy for you. And you'll marvel that all it took was someone—someone whom you thought of as brilliant and hardworking—giving you permission not to put work above everything else. And you'll wonder if Yevgeny was able to help you because, in addition to being kind and smart, he wasn't American. For despite his rapid assimilation to American language and culture, despite his willingness to work long, hard hours, Yevgeny retained one strikingly un-American trait: he was not made uncomfortable by the sadness of failure.

JANUARY 2003

Over winter break you spend seven hundred dollars of your fake violin money on a ticket back to Egypt, the country where you hope to work after graduation. You march into the Cairo office of the *New York Times* bureau chief and attempt to sweet-talk your way into a job. You mention your college course work, your Arabic language skills, your knowledge of Cairo. You even mention, shamelessly, your Appalachian childhood and its testament to your willingness to work hard, as hard as it takes, harder than anyone else in the whole damn newsroom. This conversation is only the first of many that you will have with reporters and editors in Cairo. They all unfold the same way, as if following a script:

OLDER MALE JOURNALIST WHO WORKS FOR IMPORTANT NEWS OUTLET: You'd be great. But we usually hire local Egyptians. They cost less.

JESSICA: I'll fetch coffee. Sweep floors. I'll go to Baghdad. Kabul. I'll take the most dangerous assignments. Or the shittiest ones— hot and boring places no other reporter wants to cover—Jeddah? I am tough. I have a cool head. All I need is room and board and health insurance in case I get sick or shot or blown up or whatever. You don't even have to pay me.

OLDER MALE JOURNALIST: (*Chuckling to himself*) I'll get back to you. But believe it or not, news organizations are cutting their budgets right now.

JESSICA: But there's going to be a war . . .

OLDER MALE JOURNALIST: Yes, there will be a war all right. But who will want to read about it? More to the point, who will want to *pay* to read about it? Have you heard of the Internet? The death of print journalism? This isn't a college seminar; no one cares about the political nuances of Iraqi Kurdistan. They don't care about it now, and they won't care about it once the war starts.

Fine, you think, as you walk back through Tahrir Square. You are undeterred. No skin off your back—you had started high with the

Times but you would go lower. And lower. And lower. The script replays. You return to New York and apply for a Fulbright grant to study journalism in Egypt. "You're a shoe-in," says a college dean during a meeting to discuss your application. "You'll be living in Egypt next year."

Even so, you apply for jobs around America and in the Middle East. You do so while working for The Composer each weekend, taking a full course load, and not taking drugs. You drink entire pots of coffee to stay awake and eat large slices of pizza and gain back the weight you lost. You apply for more grants. You apply for internships at the Council on Foreign Relations and *Foreign Affairs* magazine and the Washington Institute for Near East Policy. Where internships don't exist, you write letters asking for one anyway, figuring you can pay your bills by working on the weekends as a fake violinist. You research every English-language academic journal on the Middle East and send them your résumé. You apply to journalism jobs in Arkansas and Vermont and Virginia. You attend job seminars and sign up for mock interviews at the Career Center. You post your résumé on the alumni database. You attend every event you can squeeze in between working and studying so that you can make what the counselors at Career Services call "contacts."

And when you fail to hear back from any of these, you blame yourself. After all, Columbia promised to open all doors. If the doors don't open, it must be your fault. Maybe your grades aren't high enough. You made mostly As, but you do have some Bs, and one C, in Introduction to Psychology. Maybe that C is ruining everything. Maybe you don't have enough extracurricular activities. Maybe you have misspelled some crucial word in your cover letter. Maybe if you hadn't been spending nearly every weekend traveling across America playing your violin, you'd have made the right contact.

FEBRUARY 2003

"WHERE ARE WE SUPPOSED TO GO?" the woman screams at the police.

The police are on horseback, corralling the woman and you and hundreds of thousands of other war protesters into tiny, roped-off sections on side streets near the United Nations. The march— though planned in advance and with up to a million participants— has been declared "illegal" by the NYPD. The police are riding the horses through the crowd, billy clubs waving. The crowd is moving and you are moving with it, though you are too short to see over the shoulders of the people around you to determine in which direction you are being pushed. All you know is that you can feel the rib cages of the people in front and back of you. They expand and collapse with each breath, and it is only when they both collapse that you can expand your own rib cage and breathe.

The strangest thing about protesting the war—the war that has yet to even begin—is how conventional protesting a war seems. It does not feel particularly rebellious, even if it is "illegal." Even when you are almost trampled by a horse, you think to yourself, *This is just like what the old folks did, in the olden days of Vietnam!*

And yet, the vast majority of the faces around you are young faces; there are few people old enough to have marched during Vietnam. And this is disconcerting to you. For your generation is using *their* music: Jefferson Airplane, Bob Dylan, Buffalo Springfield. Your generation is chanting *their* chants: "One, two, three, four! We don't want your fucking war!" Your generation is updating *their* slogans for posters and t-shirts: "My Bush Makes Love Not War." Your generation is banging on bucket drums and burning incense because you are imitating your parents' version of a war protest.

But at this protest in 2003, the faces of your parents' generation are relatively few. Their icons—the Clintons—and their
mouthpiece—the *New York Times* editorial board—are too scared
to object to the war. The polling data are clear: the majority of the
baby boomer generation—the once-hippies, once-protesters, once-
flower children, once-tuned-in and dropped-out—are now war sup-
porters. When you express your antiwar views to one baby boomer
couple you know that spent the 1960s in a free-love commune, they
accuse you of sympathizing "with the terrorists." Even your own
father, who witnessed the shootings at Kent State, who was almost
trampled by a horse at a civil rights rally, whose peace-love-dove
values have inspired you to march at this march, even *he* now argues
with you. Perhaps the war is necessary, he says to you, his daughter,
a person who has just spent four years and a great deal of his money
learning everything she can about the Middle East, traveling to
Egypt, learning to speak Arabic. The weapons don't exist, you say.
But how do you know? The weapons are irrelevant, you say. *They won't
be irrelevant when some terrorist uses them.* The terrorists aren't from
Iraq! *How do you know?* Because they aren't!

Not that your generation is doing much better. You see two
fronts unfolding, depending on geography: Back home, in the valleys of the mountain fog, the children you grew up with are donning
camouflage and posing in the local newspaper before being shipped
off to their bases, their eyes staring out from the gray newsprint at
something in the distance—some confident, some terrified, some
so brave and resolute it's easy to forget they are teenagers. Some
believe in the beauty of America. Others believe in the beauty of an
enlistment bonus. Many signed up after 9/11 for the war in Afghanistan, a war they believed in, only to be reshuffled to Iraq, a war
they did not.

In a different land, three hundred or so miles to the north, at a marble-walled Ivy League campus sealed off from the poverty and crime just outside its iron gates, it's as if the approaching war is a mildly interesting foreign sporting event, like badminton or cricket. There are war protests and teach-ins, but apart from the ravaged city skyline, daily life on campus has not changed much since you first arrived in 1999, one major terrorism attack and two wars ago. Inside the iron gates students preoccupy themselves with other problems. The tech bubble has burst. Jobs are scarce. The less fortunate among us have large amounts of student debt. And you notice that even the most privileged students have parents tapping their toes to the rhythm of "When I was your age . . ."

We need jobs. We need health insurance. We need security deposits for apartments in New York City. We need money—two hundred dollars—for the cap and gown and diploma fees ("What?" You almost scream at the dean informing you of graduation procedures. "The diploma isn't included in the tuition?!"). We attend seminars on "How to Survive the Real World," where a man in a business suit says that the best time to start saving for retirement is *right now* and if you wait longer, you will find yourself old and poor and destitute and slurping ramen through your dentures, if you can even *afford* dentures. Meanwhile, a committee has been formed among your classmates to raise donations for the Class of 2003 Alumni Fund. You attempt to dodge them, but one committee member corners you to explain that the fund will be used "for students who can't afford to go here."

In just a few weeks, a sizable portion of your class is snapped up by large Wall Street corporations. Another portion is accepted to big-name law and medical schools. And you begin to realize that, for the past four years, you have been playing a game that you had no idea you were playing, a game in which the prize is Wall Street or Yale Law or Harvard Medical or Stanford Business, a game with prizes that you realize, too late, you never had any interest in winning.

Even so, you, along with the rest of your graduating class, all share one major prize, a prize not afforded to several people from your high school, and you struggle to comprehend the magnitude of it, the luck of it, the geography of it: none of you will be maimed or killed or psychologically destroyed in Afghanistan or Iraq.

MARCH 2003

The Iraq War, you promise yourself you will tell your grandchildren some day, was like a poisonous snake slithering across the length of a football field. Everyone could see it coming from a long distance. We could have walked away from it. We could have shot it with a round of snake-shot. We could have clubbed it over the head with a hoe. Instead, it slithered right up. It took a while, but it got there. And then it struck, lightning fast. And the venom spread. Slowly, agonizingly. For more than a decade.

And if your grandchildren ask you "What were Americans doing while the snake was slithering toward them?" you have an answer. For you saw them, thousands of Americans, in New York and Connecticut and Arkansas and Florida and Virginia and Vermont. Rich and poor, Democrat and Republican, black and white, women and men. You saw them all right, watched them for hours, and they were all doing the same thing: listening to music. They craved it, were charmed by it, hypnotized, soothed. Couldn't get enough of it. Bought twelve CDs at a time. Millions of albums. Music that sounded just like a movie about an entire society—rich on the top deck, poor on the bottom—headed for disaster.

God Bless America Tour 2004
Nashville

Harriet, Kim, and I call a taxi. A plump blonde pulls up to our hotel, sandalwood incense smoke billowing out the windows of her cab. She is pretty, but when she opens her mouth, several of the more important teeth are missing.

To the honkytonks, we say. You got it, she answers.

She is from Nashville but doesn't go out much anymore. You might be a redneck, she says, if you go to church before you go barhopping.

"It's fine to go to church and then barhop," Kim says, "as long as you don't bring anyone home afterward."

I am tempted to ask Kim which passage of the Bible mentions barhopping, but tonight I'm on my best behavior. For the first night in nearly a week, we are no longer in Cartersville, Georgia. I ate a delicious dinner of steamed vegetables that were not toppings on a Supreme pizza. The night is warm. The Nashville sky neon-lit.

The might-be-a-redneck driver takes us to Printer's Alley. We choose a place that looks suitably honkytonk and are enveloped by smoke and sweat and loud live music. A crusty middle-aged man in a cowboy hat stumbles up to me, his mustache speckled with flecks of beer foam. You look upset, he says to me, and for a moment I believe him, until I realize this is just his line. Tell a woman she's upset and maybe she'll believe you, seek comfort in your beer-soaked mustache.

He asks if he can buy me a drink. No, I'm fine, I say. But he brings me one anyway, a pink watermelon vodka shooter in a test tube that looks like something a middle-schooler might imbibe if she wanted to get drunk at a science fair. Thanks, I mumble, examining the tube in my hand like a chemist.

Meanwhile the band is taking requests. We play a mix of rock and country, they announce, but they don't actually play any country. They play the White Stripes and Godsmack and Led Zeppelin. They play "You Shook Me All Night Long" three times, until it does feel like all night long. I ask the band's leader if they could play "Chattahoochee." We crossed the Chattahoochee River earlier in the day and it made me think of middle school dances, which in my neck of the woods always involved Alan Jackson singing, *It gets hotter than a hoochie-coochie.*

"Chattahoochee," the bandleader repeats, spitting the word back at me.

"Yes?" I reply.

"Naw," he says, looking disgusted. "We wanna have fun tonight. No Chattahoochee."

"Oh, okay. Sorry," I say, taken aback by the firmness of this refusal. "I understand."

It's true. I do understand. I know what it feels like to hate a song so much you never want to hear another goddamned note.

God Bless America Tour 2004
Memphis

At our concert in Memphis, fifty expected audience members manifest as twenty, and most appear to be asleep. Almost all are in their eighties or nineties (*Um . . . guys . . . some people out there are dying . . . so you need to smile!*) and they are unusually unreceptive to the lure of the pennywhistle, or perhaps just hard of hearing. They sit motionless in their seats, staring at us with mouths agape. After the songs end Patrick has to get the applause going from the back; a few times even this doesn't work and Patrick is the only person in the room clapping. And no one could mistake Patrick as unaffiliated. He is wearing his official God Bless America Tour jacket, his arms crossed over his wide chest, tears twinkling in his eyes.

Then, right in the middle of The Composer's halftime routine (*The Hollywood Celebrity is a really cool guy!*), an elderly man arrives. I can see his black-and-white checkered pants all the way from the stage. A PBS volunteer guides him to his seat, but once there, he won't sit down. He is doing a little dance.

"WHERE'S THE MUSIC?" he yells at the top of his lungs in the middle of The Composer's speech. It's as if he thinks that if he dances, the music will follow. "WHAT'S GOING ON?"

For the first time all tour, I am genuinely smiling—a huge, honest, cancer-curing grin. The volunteer finally gets the man to sit down, just as The Composer says he worries about everyone and is praying for us all, praying for everyone to "stay safe."

"GOOD!" shouts the man.

We begin to play and the man leaps up from his chair again and begins to dance. The volunteer tries to get him to sit down but he won't.

"WOW," he yells after every song. When the concert ends, he becomes the first person in the history of The Composer's concerts to yell "WHOOPEEE!"

We leave the stage and the man bounds after us, following us into the green room, shouting after The Composer.

"YOUNG MAN, I WANT YOUR CARD!"

"Okay," The Composer says, smiling for real.

"YOUNG MAN! I WANT YOU TO COME PLAY FOR MY ROTARY CLUB!"

"All right," The Composer says, smiling not for real. Then the man begins to dance again, a little jig.

Meanwhile, another fan is following me around the backstage area. She is wearing a purple dress with a pink hat, pink purse, and pink high heels. Her eyeglasses are cat-shaped with rhinestones on the ends.

"I'm eighty-six!" she shouts at me as I pack up my violin.

"Wow!" I say.

"I've lived in my house for seventy-four years!" she shouts.

"Wow!" I say.

"Have you been to the zoo?" she answers.

"Yes!" I say, trying to keep up with the swift pace of this conversation.

"I like the pandas!" she shouts.

"That's nice!"

"They eat bamboo!"

"That's right!"

"I like music!"

"Me too!"

We extricate ourselves and load the equipment into the RV. We are ready to go, but three PBS volunteers run after us. They are carrying large aluminum trays.

"It's barbeque," they say. "From the best place in Memphis. Here are the ribs, and there's the brisket, and the pulled pork, and there are sides . . ."

Harriet and I lose our minds. We have been begging The Composer all day to stop somewhere for Memphis barbeque, but his facial expression suggested we were destined to eat a microwaved Louisiana shrimp at a Tennessee Ruby Tuesday or, more likely, a box of chicken gizzards from the Flying J, gizzards being the only hot food left at truck stops late at night.

But now an entire container of Memphis pulled pork has materialized. And green beans. Potato salad. Fresh icebox rolls, their brown tops shining with salted butter.

Ohmygod! Ohmygod! Ohmygod! Harriet and I shout. *This is so great! Thankyouthankyouthankyou!*

We are so excited that everyone else on the RV becomes excited as well, even The Composer, who won't eat any of it.

"We wanted you to have a good memory of Memphis," the PBS volunteers say.

Harriet and I strap the barbeque containers down to the countertops with duct tape. As the RV pulls away from the curb, we wave good-bye to the volunteers, our hands already dripping with BBQ sauce.

"AMERICA!" I yell at Harriet, waving a victory rib.

She laughs, and in perfect imitation of the old man, yells back "WHOOPEEE!"

God Bless America Tour 2004
Memphis to Little Rock

It's the first time I've seen the Mississippi River from the ground level, as opposed to spotting it from a plane window and using it to calculate the remaining time till landing in the West or the East. But now we're in The Middle, and the Mississippi looks like I expected it to look: big and brown. What I didn't expect is how different the country is on the other side—a flat green carpet, low and dark and wet. In America, an entire landscape can disappear in an instant.

Our final concert at Carnegie Hall is less than two months away, and my email account is full of revised contracts from The Composer's head manager, Jake. Instead of our bare-bones touring ensemble, the Carnegie Hall concert will feature all of the musicians who played on the televised God Bless America PBS special, including Yevgeny. This way it won't be so obvious that the Ensemble can mix and match musicians like socks.

Shortly after I receive my Carnegie Hall contract from Jake, I get an email from Yevgeny. It says, simply: *I quit.* Below it is a forwarded message:

Dear Jake,

I have been looking forward to the Carnegie Hall concert ever since you told me about it; but . . . my feelings have changed.

The sole purpose of this contract is to ensure that you have all the original "God Bless America" DVD musicians performing at the concert. . . . [I]t would look really bad if you pulled the usual Composer-switch—hiring all the different people to do the different type of venues.

What I'm wondering now, is: does the promoter know that none of the musicians he saw on PBS were actually playing and that the whole thing was over-dubbed? And what would he think if he found out? What would he say if he knew that The Composer didn't even play his own piano solo?

Bottom line is this: I can no longer be a part of a company

built on lies and deception . . . I am only now fully realizing
how much I hated the environment I was forced to work in,
and how much I'd have to disrespect myself . . . to perform at
this concert.

Yevgeny

After reading this in a Memphis hotel room, I call Yevgeny, but
he doesn't answer. Months later we'll meet for a drink in midtown
Manhattan. He will tell me about his new job—at an advertising
company—which he likes. He works normal hours and earns a good
salary with benefits. It's creative work, he will tell me, as if anticipat-
ing my doubt that the job is good enough for him. When I begin to
tell him about the more absurd moments of the God Bless America
Tour, he will stop me and say he doesn't want to talk about anything
related to The Composer. He doesn't even want to talk about anything related to the violin. He's left all of that behind, he will say,
and is a much happier person now.

A Single Job Offer
New York City, May 2003

Despite what could be fairly described as an enormous effort
undertaken by someone not unaccustomed to getting and holding down jobs, you are not able to find a paying job in the Middle East,
nor as a journalist, nor in any capacity that would put your hard-won,
expensive education to work for the society that had helped to fund a

large portion of it with government-subsidized student loans. In the last months of your senior year, despite sending dozens of applications to a variety of employers, you fail to receive a single job offer, a single interview, a single phone call back. A few weeks before graduation, there is a final blow: the Fulbright grant rejects you during the final round. But before you can wallow in the utter despair of all of this, there is a more pressing crisis—within just a few weeks you will have nowhere to live. The school housing system doesn't allow graduating students to stay through the month of May. Like a wayward tenant being evicted, you have twenty-four hours after graduation to vacate the campus.

And so begins one of the most challenging quests that one can undertake in New York City: the quest for affordable housing. At first you search with friends, traveling to Chinatown and the Lower East Side with Nicole, a Los Angeles native who, at the age of twenty-two, is already a successful filmmaker. Nicole knows what's up in a way you never will, and you follow her around as she sets up appointments with brokers who meet the two of you in graffitied alleyways and lead you through the rain showers of late spring to one-roomed lofts over fish markets ($3,000/month). You follow her into cramped offices where Orthodox Jewish women with gorgeous, glowing faces and long flowing skirts introduce you to the last point of civilization on Avenue D in the East Village, where a vacant four-bedroom apartment that smells of cats can be yours (if you share it with four other people) for $5,000/month. You don't get very far in this process before realizing that you—with your lack of money, and parents unaccustomed to signing guarantor statements—are the one holding things up. So you excuse yourself from the group search, and Nicole finds someone else to live with, an investment banker.

Every single one of your college friends is entering similar territory: apartments that require brokers fees, four months of security deposits, and parental guarantees requiring proof of an annual income that is, in at least one case, the total annual rent multiplied by sixty ("That's like, two million dollars," you say, before realizing you should have kept the math to yourself, after one of your friends explains the process she went through to land her apartment). Your college friends snatch up apartments at a dizzying pace—some palatial, some dingy, most unimpressive given the rent—on the Lower East Side, the Upper West, the Meat Packing District, and even, in one case, in the same building as the Stock Exchange. And so you reenter the rental market again, this time alone. You have $800 in your bank account, which makes the math simple: You can pay $400 for rent, $400 for a security deposit.

No one tells you that you'll never find an apartment in New York City for four hundred dollars. Hasidic brokers show you lofts in the far outreaches of Brooklyn where you could, theoretically, live with five other people if you all built your own walls. Recently divorced fathers on the Upper East Side display the empty rooms their children once inhabited, the floors still strewn with abandoned toys. A pot-bellied, middle-aged man wearing a wife-beater shows you a bedroom with a stained mattress in his midtown railroad apartment and casually explains that he will have to walk through your bedroom to reach the bathroom. A Portuguese woman who doesn't speak English communicates to you in gestures in a one-room basement near Lincoln Center, showing you how a bedsheet could be hung to separate her mattress from yours.

No one tells you that you can't rent an apartment in New York City for four hundred dollars, and it's lucky they don't, because in this quest, at least, you will be blessed with a stroke of such incredible luck you will shock New Yorkers at dinner parties for years: a sunny, three-bedroom apartment with a large living room and kitchen (shared with two recently arrived female immigrants from Brazil and Romania) with hardwood floors in a neighborhood that is un-chic and full of drug dealers but relatively safe. No broker's fee, no guarantor forms. Your room, large for New York, has an actual closet where you can hang your clothes. It is a room of your own, like Virginia Woolf's (although hers also came with an annual stipend and no need for employment). And it's a room that you have *found* on your own, with no help from anyone, which makes it seem doubly yours. All for the rent-stabilized price of $383/month.

As incredible as this is, it doesn't register with you at the time, for now you have handed over all but thirty-four dollars of your money in cash to a handsome Trinidadian super. You still have no job, other than your weekly gigs for The Composer, which will pay the rent for now but could end at any moment.

And so you start again, not as naïve as the young girl who first arrived in New York City. For you now know your Penn Station from your Grand Central, your express train from your local, your indoor face from your outdoor face—the "Don't fuck with me" expression every young woman in New York City eventually learns to wear.

You spend your first days in your new apartment sitting on the floor (you don't yet have any chairs) in the sun-filled living room, drinking coffee out of a new cup, applying for jobs. And it is on one of these mornings, as you sit behind a borrowed laptop, one window open to job listings in New York, Washington, D.C., and the Middle East, another window open to the latest news out of Baghdad, that Becca Belge calls you to see if you are available for a performance the following week. But this time, she's not calling about a weekend gig to a mall or a craft fair. She's calling for something much bigger. Something much better paid.

"How would you like to be on national TV?" she asks.

PART III
Watertight Compartments

You become all and only the thing you want and nothing
else, for you have paid too much for it, too much in want-
ing and too much in waiting and too much in getting.

—Robert Penn Warren, *All the King's Men*

All right boys, like the captain said, nice and cheery so
there's no panic.

—First violinist Wallace Hartley, *Titanic*

National Television

Portsmouth, New Hampshire, June 2003

As you play your violin, fourteen PBS cameramen operate seven high-definition cameras—including one that swoops back and forth over your head from a jib—getting wide-range shots of the two-tiered auditorium of the historic Portsmouth Music Hall, a venue where Mark Twain once read his work and "Buffalo Bill" Cody once performed his Wild West Show and Wynton Marsalis and Joshua Bell and David Crosby once performed music that was presumably live.

The auditorium is filled to capacity with nearly a thousand fans who are, as The Composer says, "hardcore." They are eager to participate in a televised concert special that will soon be broadcast by every major PBS station in the country and sold on DVD: *God Bless America*. The special, featuring narration by The Hollywood Celebrity, will become a nationwide PBS hit and, a year later, spark a fifty-four-city tour of America. PBS will be so pleased with the special that they will commission similar specials from The Composer in the future.

On stage in Portsmouth, The Composer's Ensemble does not look like most orchestras. There are only fourteen musicians, all with strange smiles on their faces, and the assortment of instruments is bizarre: six violinists, one flute player, three cellists, two percussionists, and The Composer at a grand piano. There is also an older, balding man at an electric keyboard, sitting in a darkened back corner, whose presence might be mystifying, unless you know that his role is to visually account for any sound that could not have been produced by the other thirteen musicians. Of course, all the sounds that the audience members actually hear in Portsmouth and later on TV were recorded years earlier, with different musicians. The stage is dimly lit and drenched in dense billowing clouds of stage fog. You can barely see past the dead microphone in front of you.

Before the concert begins, there is a dress rehearsal and sound check. Dozens of video and lighting and sound technicians run around the stage, preparing their equipment, whispering urgently to one another, barking orders into walkie-talkies. At some point one of the sound techs begins yelling frantically into his wireless headpiece. He becomes so agitated that the dress rehearsal comes to a halt.

"I don't *know!*" he yells to the control room crew. "We're not getting *anything*. ANYTHING! I can't figure it out! We've got nothing!"

Every single musician on the stage knows why the sound tech isn't "getting anything." But the only person who speaks is Kim. Still holding her pennywhistle, she walks across the stage, over to The Composer.

"Just tell them," she says softly. "Just tell them."

God Bless America Tour 2004
Little Rock

Somewhere between "Misty Lake" and "Forests of Gold" I realize that, despite going to the bathroom three times before the concert started, I have to pee. Except I don't actually have to pee. My mind is tricking me, attempting to convince me to flee the stage. I try to ignore it.

Harriet and I have a secret language on stage. We live for the small flourishes in the music, the one or two measures where The Composer's shallow compositions reach their maximum depth. But tonight I cannot relish the flourishes. I have to pee. But I do not have to pee. But how does one ever really know? How did I know before, whether or not I had to pee? When did I learn? If I can remember how I learned, maybe I can relearn. It's a thing you take for granted, knowing when to pee, a piece of knowledge that you never question until you do, and then everything in life becomes impossible (To pee or not to pee . . .). The notes march slowly across the staff paper. I fantasize about The Composer hitting the Fast-Forward button on the Sony CD player, speeding up our concert so it takes a fraction of the time. This makes me think back to my college astronomy class. According to Einstein's theory of special relativity, I could get from September to December in five minutes with the right kind of rocket ship. And what about all those quantum physics theories that suggest it's possible for an object to be in two places at the same time? Ergo: According to Einstein, I am not on this stage. According to Einstein, it is already Christmas Eve and I am back home at my parents' house in Virginia (my own bathroom!) eating the Feast of the Seven Fishes and anise cookies and wrapping presents. According to Einstein, I am not really in Little Rock, Arkansas, about to pee on stage.

Einstein doesn't work, so I try a different tactic. *Relish each note*, some fake cheerful voice inside of me says. Hit each note with the sweet spot of fingertip fat. Warm the note with vibrato. Your fingers are tiny fires, warming up notes for dinner. Next note. Hit. Sway. Warm. Twenty more measures. Fifteen. Five. Six more songs to go. Fifty measures. Thirty. Twenty. Five more songs to go. I have to pee. You do not have to pee. But it sure feels like I do. You do not. Four more songs.

I try to relax, but then I become terrified that if I relax too much I will pee. Before I left for the tour I went to three doctors, thinking I had developed a urinary tract infection. Or perhaps my symptoms had something to do with the severe and chronic intestinal illness I developed a few months before going on tour. But the doctors all came to the same conclusion: everything was normal with my bladder. My urinary symptoms had nothing to do with my intestinal illness. *It will go away*, I thought. *Nothing is wrong with me.*

It has yet to occur to me that nothing has to be wrong with one's body for one's mind to go haywire. It has yet to occur to me that the mind could play such a mean trick, going after the one thing in life I want to discuss the very least: my bathroom habits. It has yet to occur to me that there *is*, in fact, a diagnosis for this: crazy.

Crazy is what happens when one person splits into two. The first part deceives (*I* have to pee). The second part knows it's a deception (*You* don't have to pee).

You don't know it yet, but it's here at a concert in Little Rock, Arkansas, that you have your first full-blown panic attack, the first of hundreds of attacks you will experience, the opening notes of a disorder that will mar the upcoming years so completely that your life will become unrecognizable from anything you ever expected it to be. The attacks will cause you to behave in bizarre ways that you know make no sense, ways that you know make you look insane, but you cannot stop. Up until now the attacks have only been hints, vague premonitions of dread, which you chalk up to the sound of the pennywhistle. But at this concert in Little Rock the rewiring of your brain—the scrambling of the fight-or-flight instinct—escalates at an alarming speed:

Not only am I going to pee myself in front of a hundred people, I'm going to throw up. My dress is going to fall off, my shoes will break underneath me, crippling me. My knees are just a thread—how are my legs held together? Am I sure they are held together? Have I ever checked to make sure? I am going to faint. I am going to throw up and faint at the same time and then choke on my own vomit. I am going to smash my violin on the ground and stomp it with my foot. I am going to throw my violin at an audience member and start screaming obscenities. Worse than obscenities, offensive things, the most vile things I can imagine: racial slurs, September 11th was a wonderful day, fuck the veterans and fuck the elderly and fuck cute babies. Fuck abused puppies and fuck PBS. I have no control over anything, not my body, not my mind, and certainly not the musical soundtrack that is shaking the air all around me. I'm on a predestined track that can't be stopped. I am going to die up here, and no one will know because I'm smiling.

After the concert I sprint to the bathroom, slam the stall door shut, all but rip off my concert dress and underwear, and slam my butt on the toilet. It's only then that I realize: You don't have to pee. Not at all.

You Became Audible to Yourself

Years later you will read that a panic attack is a scrambling of the same flight instinct that tells the human being to run from a bear. But you'll never find that description to be accurate. The panic you experience for the first time on stage in Little Rock is not like the panic you'd feel if you were being chased by a bear. No, it is, instead, like the panic you'd feel once the bear has already caught you and has begun to eat you, the panic of someone with no chance of survival, in the last moments of consciousness, when neither fight nor flight will help.

Your panic attacks escalate, as panic attacks do, though you don't know anything about panic attacks when you first begin having them on the God Bless America Tour. In time the attacks will invade every area of your life until you cannot ride airplanes or subways or elevators or cars or be anywhere that doesn't offer immediate access to an unoccupied bathroom. (And even immediate access to a bathroom doesn't always count as a safe place. *How many times are you allowed to get up during a movie?* you ask yourself. *How many times during a friend's wedding?* You parcel your life into thirty-minute segments, the maximum amount of time you can convince yourself that you won't pee yourself, though you never actually need to pee.) Sometimes even your own parents (who will take care of you for months after you return from the tour and pay for your health insurance so that you can see a psychiatrist) are too large an audience for you to handle, and you hide in their basement where no one in the world can see you, reading books and playing Mario 1 on your brother's ancient Nintendo set, which hasn't been hooked up since you were in seventh grade.

Part of the problem is the embarrassment. You do not want to talk about having to pee. It is gross, and no one wants to be gross, especially not a young woman still trying to reconcile *life in the body*. Later, you will find out that panic attacks disproportionately afflict young women in their twenties. Later, your dad will invite you to shadow him on a night shift in the emergency room for an article you are writing, and you will discover the ER at three o'clock in the morning is not full of blood and gore but women in their twenties having panic attacks. There is a particular, feminine shame in the act of crying "I'm dying" when nothing is actually wrong. Panic attacks serve as confirmation of the very things women spend their lives working to negate: suspicions of female silliness, stupidity, hysteria. Panic attacks involve the removal of the mind's control over the body, and in this way are aftershocks of an earlier mind-body separation—the moment when adolescent girls realize that no amount of brains or charm will save them from *life in the body*.

You will also find out later that there is an entire subset of psychiatric disorders that revolve around the fear of losing control of one's bodily fluids. You feel a powerful kinship with the *Atlantic* editor Scott Stossel, who writes about an emetophobia so powerful that he bolts out of an interview with Bill Clinton, convinced that he is moments away from vomiting on the president, only to realize, after he flees, that he feels perfectly fine.

At the core of any anxiety is fear, and yours is this: You have lost control over everything. The differences between the real and the fake are beginning to blur, not just in your mind, but in your actual body. You have spent years working hard under the belief that hard work matters, but you are suddenly struck by the idea that *nothing* you do matters—because everything is fake. You look up the price of health insurance premiums for a woman your age with a preexisting condition. The sums are significantly more than your rent, more than your ballooning student loan payments that you have already placed in deferment. You realize you are not going to be able to use the money you are making from the God Bless America Tour to return to the Middle East and become a war correspondent, as had been your original plan. You are not going to be able to make a living doing anything remotely interesting or important or artistic or special. You are going to sink to the bottom. It is a mathematical certainty.

In his *New Yorker* article titled "Petrified," John Lahr writes that performers who experience stage fright feel exposed, at sudden risk for losing control of the body. Lahr points out that "break a leg" and "merde" are good-luck sayings that recognize the risk of making a bodily mess on stage. "Instead of being protected, as usual, by the character he is playing," Lahr writes, the performer "suddenly stands helpless before the audience as himself; he loses the illusion of invisibility."

But perhaps visual metaphors are the wrong way to describe what happens to you, a musician. If actors lose "the illusion of invisibility," you lose the illusion of silence. You suddenly *hear* yourself. And you do not sound like the Vivaldi you played in your head at four years old. Despite ten years of lessons, you still can't play all the notes in Vivaldi's "Winter," which has a fast tempo and a challenging key signature.

No, you do not sound like Vivaldi. You do not sound like a

creeping mountain fog. You do not sound like the seriousness of life and death.

You sound like *Titanic*.

God Bless America Tour 2004
Little Rock to Baton Rouge

W e speed south into pitch-black Arkansas on a rural route. Around two in the morning, we stop at an old house, a bed and breakfast. Harriet and I carry our suitcases up creaking stairs and collapse onto four-poster beds with scratchy quilts. A few hours later, milky sunlight streams through antique lace curtains and, half-awake, I reach for the phone book on the nightstand. But there is no nightstand, no phone book, and I fall back asleep not knowing where I am.

The next day we drive past dark pools of water with puffs of cotton floating on their surfaces and arthritic trees reaching out of their depths. I rummage past the I-should-be-reading-this books in my RV cubby and go straight to my emergency books, the ones that I have brought on this tour precisely because I have read them a million times already and they can be counted on to take me somewhere else, anywhere besides where I am. At first I consider rereading *Pride and Prejudice*. But something about the way the trees look outside the window makes me want to reread *All the King's Men*.

The America Robert Penn Warren describes is so different, yet so similar to the one I see outside the RV window: *There were pine forests here a long time ago but they are gone. The bastards got in here and set up the mills* (The Walmarts, I think as we fly through Louisiana towns blighted by strip malls. The Ruby Tuesdays, the Hampton Inns) . . . *and paid a dollar a day and folks swarmed out of the brush for the dollar* . . . *The saws sang soprano* (the pennywhistle, I think) *and the clerk in the commissary passed out the blackstrap molasses and the sowbelly* (Frosties and McRibs) . . . *Till, all of a sudden, there weren't any more pine trees* . . . *There wasn't any more dollar a day. The big boys were gone, with diamond rings on their fingers and broadcloth on their backs* (what this place will look like when Walmart, having sucked the marrow out of the bones of small-town businesses, finally shuts its doors as well, I think, looking out at a Louisiana town that's all but dead, its only pulse a skinny blue-vested teenager pushing a bumpy line of empty shopping carts toward the immaculate glass doors, which yawn open and swallow him whole).

In the beginning of the book, the narrator Jack Burden offers his sardonic descriptions of Willie Stark, who we know is really the politician Huey Long, without taking any responsibility for his own life. (That comes later.) But in the beginning, Jack Burden describes Stark from a distance, while Willie's on stage. And even though this happens in the first few pages, we the readers already know that Willie Stark is a master of deceiving his audience. He gives a speech about how he's not giving a speech, and the crowd of bumpkins, not realizing that they've been had, loves it.

As I take turns reading and staring out the RV's dinette window at a landscape dotted with cotton puffs and mobile homes, The Composer stumbles and bangs his way from his back room to the driver's seat, where he asks Patrick some variation on are-we-there-yet. Now that he has finished his Christian musical he has more time on his hands. He's reading a book, too—the seafaring adventure novel *Master and Commander.* He saw the movie with Russell

Crowe and loved it so much he decided to read the book. When I ask him if the book is good, he says it is, that he likes books about boats. And then he tells me about life at sea, how hard it was for the sailors, and that the master and commander is just another name for the captain of the ship.

"And what's cool about the Master and Commander," he says with excitement, "is that he can kill anyone he wants. Like, if anyone on the boat gives him trouble, the Master and Commander can kill them."

I watch The Composer as he stands in the patch of empty space between the driver's seat and the passenger's seat talking to Patrick. He stretches his wiry arms out wide so that his hands can grasp the back of the headrests and hold himself steady on the bumpy road. The gray light through the front windshield casts a shadow so that, from where I sit, The Composer is nothing but a black silhouette in the crucifixion pose, hurtling through the Louisiana sky.

One Night, Everyone in the RV Watches *Master and Commander*

When The Composer tells me about his love for *Master and Commander*, I assume that the soundtrack for the movie includes a lot of pennywhistle. But the movie is actually all strings, most captivatingly Ralph Vaughan Williams's *Fantasia on a Theme by Thomas Tallis*. It swells up repeatedly during the movie's emotional climaxes.

When he wrote the piece in 1910, Vaughan Williams instructed the performance to include three different string orchestras seated apart from one another (large, small, smaller) like aural Russian nesting dolls. The piece is a wise selection for a movie about a ship at sea (ocean, boat, person—large, small, smaller). During one climactic swell, a little over two minutes into the piece, a small section of second violins breaks off from the larger orchestra, running arpeggios against the rest of the orchestra, which holds sustained notes of the main melody at full blast. The second violins are like a small boat fighting against a high sea. You can barely hear them—they are slurring two notes to a bow, up down up down—but they are there.

The second violinists are the least talented violinists in the orchestra, the ones who aren't as good as the first violinists in auditions, the ones whose faces you can't see even if you have a good seat. But Vaughan Williams gives them the rebellion, the countermelody that gives everything else its depth. It's their smallness that makes the entire piece of music seem immense, the way the ocean becomes larger once you see how tiny an ocean liner looks in the middle of it. It's the exact opposite effect of a composition by The Composer, which is crowded with a singular simple phrase, like a surfboard in a bathtub.

Master and Commander is as manly of a manly-men-at-war-at-sea-movie as you can get (a woman's face appears on screen just once, for about two seconds), with Russell Crowe in his full bulbous macho glory, and I have a hard time becoming involved in the story until all of a sudden, Russell Crowe, the master and commander himself, is playing a violin.

I know what this means. The ability to play classical music is cinematic shorthand for brains, competence, and sophistication. (Chess playing is another commonly used shorthand. The protagonist plays chess, ergo the protagonist is smart.) And this is doubtless what the shorthand is in *Master and Commander*. Crowe's character—Captain "Lucky Jack" Aubrey—is smart because in addition to his naval warfare skills, he plays beautiful classical music on the violin.

Except that Russell Crowe is most definitely *not* playing the violin. The first giveaway is the audio, which doesn't match what a violin would sound like in a small wooden room of a ship. More egregiously, in one crucial shot, Russell Crowe doesn't even bother to move the fingers on his left hand. And during a pizzicato section of the music, Crowe's plucking finger is nowhere near the strings.

It occurs to me at some point during the movie that this is a big-budget production ($150 million, I'll find out later). There are frighteningly believable scenes of nineteenth-century naval warfare, an astounding replica of a ship in a hurricane-force storm complete with a churning ocean, and dead-on sound effects of howling wind and cracking wood. And yet, to have Russell Crowe fake-play a violin in an even half-convincing manner has escaped Hollywood's finest technicians. Oh, sure, they cut the shot away from Crowe's fingers real quick. But in the end any amateur musician can see that the violin scenes are fake. And it's not so much because of Crowe's immobile fingers but in the way he holds the violin. He cradles it too tightly to his body, as if he is afraid he will drop it, like a father with a newborn baby. It's the universal pose of nonviolinists; every single person who has ever asked to try a few notes on my violin has become visibly frightened once I actually hand it to them. It's lighter than they expect, and they realize just how delicate it is. They marvel that something so insubstantial can produce such a weighty sound—a sound so closely resembling a full-throated human voice. They are unnerved by the combination of fragility and power. Just holding a violin can make the most macho Hollywood actor look vulnerable.

And if you don't look closely, the violin can make the most panic-stricken young woman appear to be as strong as a sea captain.

An Easy Person to Work With
New York City, August 2003

After filming the God Bless America PBS special, you go right back to applying for jobs from the sun-drenched living room of your new apartment, which now has a grape-colored couch that you found in a garbage heap on the street. The couch's cushions are missing and it has wacky arms that look like the nubs of black telephone poles, but it doesn't smell bad and isn't infested with bugs, so you consider it worth the muscle it took you and a friend to wrangle it into the elevator. You sit on the purple couch with telephone-pole arms and type cover letter after cover letter. The goal is to get a job writing in the Middle East, but at this point you'll take pretty much anything. You get your first cell phone and stare at it, waiting for your future to call you.

And then one day, after a few months of applying for jobs while paying your rent with Ensemble gig money, you do get a job (or rather, a paid internship, which to you is the same thing), in journalism. At the *New York Times*. The woman on the phone asks you to come to the office for an interview, and you race to the Chelsea address she gives you. When you arrive, you realize that this is not the address of the *New York Times*. But whatever, who knows how this stuff works.

The woman is in her late fifties and dressed in tailored designer clothing, every strand of her hair so perfectly placed that you wonder whether she is wearing a wig. You'll later find out that she was once the editor in chief of a famous fashion magazine, which is exactly the part she looks. She sits behind a large, immaculate desk that has a box of Kleenex and antibacterial lotion positioned on the corner just so. Everything—from the pens in her penholder to the perfect stack of legal pads to the gleaming canister of paper clips—looks as if it has been arranged for a photo shoot of chic office life. She explains to you that her company contracts out "special projects" for the magazine section of the *Times*. You're not quite sure what "special projects" means, but what you envision, gleefully, is assisting with Pulitzer-winning long-form journalism. She asks you if you are interested in fashion. You are not, but you know your way around an H&M well enough to pass as someone who does, or so you think, until she looks you up and down and you realize you haven't fooled her.

A few days later she calls you back to offer you the job—a three-month internship that pays double minimum wage and will be enough, with your Ensemble gigs, to pay the rent and the utilities and have enough left over for your student loan payments. She emphasizes that if you take the internship (as if you are in any danger of refusing it), you will be able to put the *New York Times* on your future résumé; of course, you know that the future résumé is the whole point of this operation, that it might be your ticket to a full-time job at the *Times* or in the Middle East or both. You also know that many successful female reporters first do time in fashion—that as a woman your only way into a newsroom might be through the Style section. When you arrive at the office the next day, she hands you a press badge, which you grab from her as if it's a winning lottery ticket. It says Jessica Hindman, Editorial, *New York*

Times. If you had owned a camera, you would have taken a picture of it and sent it home to your parents, or maybe even your local hometown newspaper, which was fond of covering any story in which the town's "youth" were up to something besides selling crystal meth or shipping off to Iraq.

It takes you a few days to realize that, press badge aside, you are not working for the *New York Times.* The "special sections" that your new company produces are advertorial inserts, glossier and better-produced versions of the grocery store coupons that fall out of your hometown newspaper. Your job is to help with the logistics of fashion shoots wherein models pose with designer merchandise, although you spend a good portion of your day merely stapling things. And sometimes unstapling them and restapling. ("In the magazine world," your boss lectures, "everything must be vertically stapled." She gestures at a stack of one thousand incorrectly stapled documents. "You'll need to redo all of this.") You realize that when your boss emphasized that you could put the *New York Times* on your résumé she had left off the last part of the sentence: "even though you won't actually work there or help to produce anything published by it."

And so you spend three months stapling and unstapling and ordering lunches and coordinating the shipment of various designer items to various fashion shoots in the West Village. You work with your boss and one other intern and never meet a single person who works for the *Times.*

But one day, she does offer you something valuable. It's nine o'clock on a Friday night and you've been in the office stapling and unstapling for twelve hours. The other intern—who lives in her parents' brownstone on the Upper West Side and comes to work every day in tailored silk blouses and pleated pants and a rotating array of designer handbags (which makes you look even more the ragamuffin, with your fifteen-dollar red clunky Mary Janes from T.J. Maxx, which you thought were hip but your boss calls "circus inspired" and adds that you might have better luck shopping at Club Monaco)—has gone home in a huff, unable to hide her exhaustion and outright disdain for your boss.

"It's late," your boss says. "Will you be able to get home all right?"

This is surprising, for she rarely asks anything about your life outside of the office. You tell her you'll be fine.

Your boss watches you as you continue to sit on the floor, unstapling, stapling. She has a strange expression on her face, as if she has been surprised by something.

"I don't normally say this," she says. "Not before someone has finished interning for me. But you . . ." She pauses, as if searching for the right words. "You are a very easy person to work with."

"Thank you," you say, beaming. And the compliment sticks with you because your boss is not the sort of person to give one easily. It sticks with you because even though you have no interest in doing what she does for a living, you respect her for who she is and are grateful for a compliment from someone like her, a successful woman from a generation of women who had to fight even harder than you do.

But years later you will look back on this moment and realize that perhaps her words were meant less as a compliment and more as a warning. Yes, you were "a very easy person to work with"—The Composer thought so, too. But perhaps this had less to do with some winsome personality trait and more to do with your pliability, your utter desperation to succeed, your need to be loved by your superiors, no matter how ridiculous or ill-advised or fraudulent the thing was that they were asking you to do.

God Bless America Tour 2004
New Orleans

I sit on a park bench under a swamp tree—one of those huge trees in New Orleans covered in moss—eating a rainbow snowball in the warm afternoon breeze, and I think: *I could quit.* Stroll down this sidewalk with my dripping snowball and never turn back. Get a job serving pitchers of beer in some New Orleans dive. What is that Bob Dylan song? Work for a while on a fishing boat right outside of Delacroix? That, I think. I could do that. Maybe if I worked on the water I wouldn't have to worry about having to pee all the time. If I really had to pee (you don't have to pee) I could just pee while treading water on the side of the boat.

The New Orleans PBS station surprises us with an extravagant reception. There is shrimp étouffée, a silver platter of frog-shaped artisan chocolates, bouquets of fresh roses, and so much champagne that they insist we take an entire case of it with us, along with a set of glass champagne flutes, an offering that Kim, Harriet, and I gladly accept. The Composer makes us give it back, saying he doesn't want alcohol in the RV. We sulk. But losing a case of free champagne is the least of my problems. I can no longer make it through the entire seventy-five minutes of the concert. I have begun to flee the stage during The Composer's halftime speech, run to a bathroom to pee (I don't have to pee) and then run back, just in time for The Composer's closing line: "I worry about all of you out there and will pray for you tonight to stay safe." (After the concert, the champagne toasts begin and we gorge ourselves on shrimp and chocolate in the rose-filled reception room of the WYES station. In less than a year, it will be underwater.)

Some part of me expects to be fired for running off the stage. It would be reasonable for The Composer to demand a violinist who can make it through a seventy-five-minute concert without fleeing the stage in terror. But The Composer, who fails to accommodate basic requests like stops for dinner and cases of free champagne, is wholly compassionate toward my plight, which I struggle to explain to him and everyone else. He doesn't interrogate me for details or ask why I'm acting like a crazy person, or, worse, accuse me of actually being a crazy person, though this is, without a doubt, what I have become. He just looks at me with the same look he gives the brassy-haired, middle-aged women who listen to his music, women who work two jobs because their husbands have died of cancer, women whose sons have died in car accidents, women who feel so anxious after a day of teaching special ed or nursing Alzheimer's patients or taking shit from the boss that they live for that moment in the car after work, the moment they turn on the CD player and take a deep breath. The Composer looks at me the way he looks at these women and seems to understand exactly what it is that I'm going through, even though I can't understand it myself.

But unlike the women at our concerts, relaxing music is not my method of choice for unwinding at the end of my day. Relaxing music is the opposite of relaxing for me. Relaxing music gives me panic attacks. I make a mental note to put it on my medical charts should I ever need surgery or fall into a coma—Patient Has Lethal Allergy to Relaxation Music—just in case the hospital pipes The Composer's music through the corridors and recovery rooms, as many of them do. I try the other obvious methods: deep breathing, exercise, yoga stretches, long walks, showers, reading, zoning out to the TV, and, when all else fails, a glass of merlot with a three-cigarette chaser (by the end of the tour, three glasses of merlot with a nine-cigarette chaser). Nothing works. My mind is a CD player with a broken Fast-Forward button, thoughts flying by faster than I can hear them, zooming past any restful pause.

I could quit. I could call Jake, the manager, tell him I have a medical emergency, give him a few days to find a replacement violinist, then flee to the safety of my parents' house in Virginia. It's true that I'm under contract, but health is health, I reason, emergencies are emergencies. Jake would probably understand. The Composer would definitely understand.

But I don't quit. There's the money to consider, for one thing. For the entire eleven-week tour, I'm contracted to receive a four-figure sum that sounds so large to me it might as well be millions of dollars. (Six months later, when doing my taxes, I'll realize that after the money is taxed and expenses deducted, I earned three thousand dollars for the three-month tour.)

More than anything, I tell myself that getting paid to tour around America as a violinist is exactly what I wanted to do when I was a kid. I tell myself that at this very minute, a zillion teenage violinists in rural America are practicing their hearts out, fantasizing about doing what I'm doing right now. And now here I am, and I'm not going to quit.

Do You Know What's Missing in This Book?

"Do you know what's missing in this book?" a writer friend asks me.

"What?"

"The guy," she says.

"The guy?" I ask. "Do you mean The Composer?"

"No, silly," she says. "The *guy*. The nice, handsome, well-educated boyfriend who makes you see that your career with The Composer is dumb and a waste of time. The one who cures your panic attacks by telling you to stop being such a self-destructive workaholic idiot. The one who inspires you to get down with the things in life that really matter, like marrying him and having his babies and moving to the suburbs and coaching swim team. You know, *the guy*. He should be making his appearance in this book right about now."

"The guy?" I say. "There is no guy. I mean, excuse me. Spoiler Alert: There is no guy."

"Come on," she says. "There's always a guy in books like this."

"What do you mean books like *this*?" I say, huffily. "Books about ambitious, artistic-minded women from small towns who are attempting to follow their dreams in New York City?"

"Exactly," she says. "Maybe you could make one up."

"I'm not going to make one up!" I say. "I'm sorry to disappoint, but I figured out that my career with The Composer was dumb all by myself. I didn't need a guy to tell me! Plus, as I'm trying to demonstrate, fake-playing the violin isn't so much of a career as it is a metaphor for—"

"At the very least put in some fucking."

"Fucking?"

"You're fucking people during all of this, right? I mean you were in your early twenties, living in New York City. Maybe you can put some of that in."

"Sure, I was fucking people, but none of those people were The Composer! And goddammit! This book is difficult enough to write without worrying about fucking, for fuck's sake! Imagine if poor George Orwell had to include all the fucking he was doing while fighting the Spanish fascists!"

"That book would be better if there was more fucking," my friend says.

"How about this," I say. "I'll include this very conversation in the book, with some major editing so that we both sound more clever and succinct than we actually are, and then the book will include both 'the guy' and 'fucking' and we can all check those things off of our lists for elements needed in books about young, career-minded women in New York City. Then we can all move on."

"It's your book," she says.

"Fucking right it is."

Thousands per Minute

December 2003

When the God Bless America special airs on PBS stations across the nation, a few months after it was shot in New Hampshire, people in your hometown begin to spread the Good News, send good tidings, speak the Good Word that is rural American Gospel:

I saw you on TV.

For there you are, in your black concert dress and your violin. You are on TV. Following your dreams. For you have a reeyell gift.

But it isn't until you begin to appear live on the home shopping channel QVC that the folks back home really begin to take notice. The Composer's first few appearances on QVC are tests: You appear on the channel at times like 3:30 in the morning, 4:17 in the morning, 2:37 in the morning. These are the times assigned to newbies; if The Composer can sell a certain number of CDs at 3:30 in the morning, he'll be invited back for primetime. So you set your alarm for 2:30 a.m. and wake up in a Pennsylvania hotel. You are shuffled into QVC's studios and onto a set that looks like a cross between David Letterman's stage and a suburban living room. You play your violin (in front of a dead microphone while the CD does the work) and are beamed out live across America. A few seconds go by. Then dozens, then hundreds, then thousands of people begin ordering CDs.

In between songs the poofy-haired, Christmas-sweatered QVC host gushes how beautiful, how soothing, how relaxing this music is. And at this special price, she asks, why not order multiple sets of CDs and give them away as Christmas presents? Who wouldn't love this music? And they are all original compositions, folks, by this composer, this *American* composer, folks, this handsome wonderful man standing right here. And The Composer smiles his goofy smile and says he is truly blessed and prays that his music will touch people's hearts and prays that everyone who is listening will be blessed, as he is. And calls come in with testimonials of how The Composer's music has cured the caller's cancer, asthma, sadness, general malaise. The calls come in saying the music is beautiful and wonderful and good.

And as you play your violin you watch the sales numbers on a monitor, thousands per minute, see exactly which high notes on the pennywhistle cause the most calls to come in. The sales rise and fall with the music, and the money rolls in, and The Composer is moved to primetime, and you play while watching the sales numbers rise.

The up and down of the sales monitor mimics the up and down of the notes on your sheet music until they seem like one, a national symphony of commerce, the most authentic-sounding American music of all.

God Bless America Tour 2004
San Antonio

The Composer's legs dangle out the passenger-side window of the RV, his body jackknifed on the window ledge. The door to the RV is jammed, so with the strength of a gymnast The Composer has pulled his entire body up through the window. The rest of us stand outside the RV in our concert clothes, holding our instrument cases. A hardcore fan has followed us from the concert reception to the parking lot. "You play that flute really well," he is saying to Kim. Patrick wears his official God Bless America Tour jacket even in the sweltering Texas air. His arms are folded across his chest as he stares skeptically at The Composer's derriere, wiggling through the open window in the evening twilight.

The jammed door is only the latest item on a growing list of our RV's maladies. The side mirrors keep falling off and dangling dangerously in the breeze while we are driving, despite Patrick's repeated attempts to hold them on with duct tape. The air vents in The Composer's back room overheat, canceling the meager effects of the dying air-conditioning system. The DVD player and radio are both broken; our days of group movie watching long past, along with our ability to tune in to the traffic and weather stations. The catch-locks on the kitchen cabinets and refrigerator are so shot that even with duct tape the doors fly open without warning; apples fall out of the sky and boxes of Cap'n Crunch sail through the air, covering us in peanut-butter-scented dust. The walls are filthy with six weeks' worth of splattered food, the trash can smells bad even when it's empty, and the linoleum beneath our feet is so sticky that we no longer worry about slipping and falling while the RV is in motion, so securely are the bottoms of our shoes fastened to the floor.

The Composer hoists the rest of his body through the window and emerges through the jammed door a few seconds later. We troop inside while the hardcore fan stands in the parking lot, waving as Patrick puts the RV in reverse. Suddenly, the back end of the RV crashes into something hard and unmoving, throwing all of us onto the cereal-encrusted floor.

We tumble back out of the RV to inspect the damage, wondering what on earth could have caused so hard a crash. It doesn't take long to figure it out; there is a cavernous ditch between the parking lot and the road, causing the back end of the cabin to smash into the asphalt. Our RV hasn't crashed into any obstacle on the road; it has crashed into the road itself.

Patrick attempts to back the RV out at a different angle but only succeeds in banging into the asphalt a few more times. It becomes clear that we will need to build a bridge over the ditch. The hardcore fan points to a pile of rubble in the parking lot, full of bricks, fruit crates, cardboard, and trash. We tote all of this by hand and fling it into the ditch, until the parking lot is level with the road. The first bridge we make isn't high enough, and the RV crashes right through it to the pavement again. We build a second bridge and Kim runs out onto the road to stop traffic while Patrick revs the engine. Then, like an elephant breaking free of its circus tent, our RV roars out of the San Antonio PBS parking lot. As we wave good-bye to the hardcore fan, we are grateful for our RV. Perhaps it's because we all share a certain need to remove ourselves from the scene of our concert crimes as quickly as possible, but our RV, despite its many problems, has begun to feel like a home.

God Bless America Tour 2004

Dallas

The club—really a poolside lounge at one of Dallas's fanciest hotels—is full of blondes dripping with diamonds, their faces glowing with the flawless, glossy finish that can only be achieved by an hour-long sit-down with a professional makeup artist, their breasts sculpted into tanned teardrops by the best surgeons oil money can buy. One particularly stunning specimen—standing at least six feet tall, her perfectly proportioned legs, hips, and breasts accentuating the tailor cut of her red blazer and skirt suit—strides across the open courtyard in sling-back stilettos, puffing on a cigar with bee-stung red lips. A man in a business suit finds her, pulls her away from the crowd by the hand.

I sit at a lounge table with Harriet and her friend Carol, a top violinist in the Dallas Symphony Orchestra, who picked us up from our suburban hotel and squired us away to Dallas splendor in her shiny new BMW. While Harriet and Carol catch up, I try to smooth my wild hair into something less Unabomber-esque. Other than my concert dress, I didn't pack any fancy clothes for the tour. I sit in the midst of the lavish Dallas scene wearing corduroy pants that have been rip-hemmed at the waist and ankles. Even with the rip-hem, the pants are much too long on me and I step on them a lot in the RV; the bottoms are filthy scraps of disintegrating corduroy, barely concealing the plastic American-flag flip-flops I bought at a JC Penney four years earlier.

Harriet and Carol reminisce about past orchestras they've played in and swap gossip on the elite classical music world: which violinist is sleeping with which bassoonist, which cellist lost his mind and stormed out of rehearsal cursing a famous conductor. Carol is in her midthirties and has short hair that accentuates her heart-shaped face and hazel eyes. I've never hung out with a professional classical musician of her caliber, and I'm in awe.

Carol is complaining to Harriet about the Dallas Orchestra's season program. "They are doing all this nonsense to build their endowment," Carol says. "They think all an orchestra needs to become top-tier is money, but the problem is that you can't buy taste. It's one thing to shamelessly insert Eine Kleine Nachtmusik into half the concerts or to go overboard on the Beethoven. But the *I Love Lucy* theme song? *The Looney Tunes* soundtrack? That's just messed up."

Harriet nods sympathetically. "That's right, that's right," she says.

"We should not have to be playing Pink Floyd to get an audience," Carol continues. "Next thing I know there's going to be a laser show going on in the concert hall and teenagers will be in the box seats dropping acid. I did not spend my life getting this good to play soundtrack music."

"Soundtrack music," I repeat. I'm not sure if I mean it as a question.

"Yeah," Carol says, looking at me with a wry expression. "My job is nothing like what you probably think it is."

God Bless America Tour 2004
Dallas to Albuquerque

You don't notice it at first. You look out the window one moment and the country is as flat and hot and crowded as a Thomas Friedman column. But then, somewhere a few hours west of Dallas, you look again, more closely this time. There are fewer cars, then very few, then you are, as far as you can tell, a passenger aboard a single vessel sailing on an open sea, with nothing in sight but hundreds of miles of empty space. There are no Ruby Tuesdays, no Walmarts, no strip malls, no truck stops full of chicken gizzard buffets. The land birds of interstate travel that signify nearby islands of restaurants and gas stations—sandwich wrappers and soda cans and plastic bags—disappear. Some muscle between your lungs and your stomach loosens, and you are able to take a deep breath for what seems like the first time since the tour began. You become something both smaller and larger at once. There is plenty of space, you think. Plenty of space for us all in this land that stretches all the way to the dark-silver horizon. After six weeks on the road in which you have seen the same landscape over and over and over again, from Maine to Georgia to Arkansas (Walmart, Lowe's, Cracker Barrel, repeat, repeat, repeat), you are unspeakably relieved to look out the window and see that this America—the empty, the uninhabited, the West—is still here.

Somewhere in the background you hear The Composer ask Harriet, "What is Barcelona?" and for a moment, just before you make a mental note to mock this question with Harriet later in your hotel room (*It's a major city in Spain, you doofus!*), you pause to marvel at the question's Whitman-esque quality: What *is* Barcelona? What is America? What is the West? What is the desert? What is the sky? What is this emptiness? *A child said, What is the grass?*

God Bless America Tour 2004

Phoenix to San Diego

A few days after The Composer asks Harriet "What is Barcelona?" he asks me "Who is John Kerry?" The RV is parked in a cactus-dappled desert a few hours from Phoenix, in front of Chee's Indian Store ("1–2–3 Say Chee's," the billboards say). Harriet and I have bought beaded earrings and fry bread.

I look at The Composer and say, "John Kerry is running for president," and The Composer nods solemnly, as if, six weeks before election day, I have imparted rare knowledge.

"Who do you think will win?" The Composer asks me.

"John Kerry," I say, fingering my new earrings. "Bush started an unnecessary war. People are going to judge him harshly for that. It will be hard for him to win after starting a war for no reason."

"It wasn't for no reason," Kim pipes up. "The terrorists—"

"There weren't any terrorists in Iraq!" I interrupt her. "Iraq is not Afghanistan. Or Saudi Arabia, where most of the 9/11 hijackers were from."

"But Saddam Hussein . . ." she continues.

"You can't just invade a country for some made-up, imaginary reason," I argue.

"Says the white girl wearing Indian beads," Harriet says.

"Isn't it true," The Composer asks, trying to change the subject, "that if you run for president, you're always on the road?"

It is true, though until The Composer mentions it, I hadn't ever considered it. Now I begin to notice that the God Bless America Tour is increasingly crisscrossing paths with both campaigns. And as someone who has been on the road nonstop for seven weeks, I begin to feel an affinity with both candidates. They wake up every day in a strange place, I think, eating strange food, sleeping very little. Their audiences, like our audiences, come from work or home, our performances a break in their daily routines. But for those of us touring America, there is no daily routine. There are no day jobs, house keys, dog walks. No homemade casseroles. There is no set bedtime, no familiar face on the local news, no houseplant to water. Every night we sleep in different beds and every morning we wake up and look at a different clock, set to a different time zone. The same invisible army that puts a *USA Today* under my hotel door and stocks the bathroom with fresh towels does the same for the president and his challenger. And, in a way, we are all selling the same thing: Listen to us, we say, and you will feel safer and calmer, more relaxed in a world full of unspeakable dangers.

That night at our concert in San Diego, I look out at the audience's faces as they watch the bald eagle swoop over the Grand Canyon. The Composer's *Titanic* music swells in the background. There is something sinister about that eagle, I think. Something unsettling about the way such an image soothes people's nerves from coast to coast.

After the concert I watch the first debate of the 2004 presidential election in my San Diego hotel room. The first question of the evening is directed toward John Kerry: *Do you believe you could do a better job than President Bush in preventing another 9/11-type terrorist attack on the United States?* Kerry answers like a groom at a wedding: *I do.* President Bush offers his rebuttal and the ceremony continues until it culminates in them shaking hands and fake-smiling and telling each other "good job." *1–2–3 Say Chee's,* I think.

Years later I'll look back on the politics of the post–September 11th years as set to the soothing melodies of the pennywhistle. John Kerry, George W. Bush, The Composer—all are like the principal violinist on the deck of the sinking *Titanic,* who instructs the players: "Nice and cheery, so there's no panic." When the violinist's body was found in the ocean a few days after the disaster, his violin case was still strapped to his back.

The Geography of Music
Buffalo, New York, 2003

M usic can shape geography. It can transform a landscape from something forgetful into something memorable.

For instance, I'll remember driving around the outskirts of Buffalo on a craft fair gig with Debbie, the red-haired flutist from the first gig in New Hampshire, and Morris, a socially awkward violinist. All weekend Morris will insist that we listen to sixteenth-century Spanish court music, compositions that were written and performed for Ferdinand and Isabella. It's the music that greeted Columbus when he went to pitch his potential investors on an innovative sea route that would lead to Asia's endless gold.

"This album has been re-mastered," Morris explains, and goes into the technical details of recording Renaissance music, the instruments, the proper acoustical venues, the recording equipment. Morris's favorite track on the CD is a vocal ballad called "Rodrigo Martinez." Morris turns it up to full volume and puts it on repeat. As we drive, gas stations and cow fields and suburban developments fly by, and the stately court music—with its trumpets and flutes and tambourines and the strong catchy beat of bass drums—transforms, like magic, the grim upstate wastelands of late-capitalism into majestic, pastoral vistas. The strip malls are timeless. The trailer parks are quaint villages. The abandoned gas stations are castles.

"It sounds like they're singing Rodrigo My Penis," Debbie points out. And once she says it, it becomes impossible to hear anything else. The old-Spanish consonants are so soft that when they are sung a "t" sounds like a "p."

"Rodrigo My Penis!" Debbie and I sing in gleeful fake baritones as we sail through Buffalo, until Morris becomes so agitated that he turns off the music.

But for years afterward the song will stay in my head. I'll eventually download it and listen to it again, and when I do I'll remember what upstate New York looked and felt like on a cold autumn weekend in 2003. I'll remember the particular feeling I used to get after a long day at an Ensemble gig, a feeling of freedom, the wonderful liberty of listening to something—anything—other than The Composer's music.

One day I become curious and look up the translation of the song's lyrics. It turns out that Rodrigo Martinez/My Penis is a Spanish madman who believes his geese are his oxen, confusing animals who make music for animals who perform hard labor:

Rodrigo Martinez, he's after the geese again, Hey!
He thinks they are his oxen, so he whistles at them, Hey!

Rodrigo Martinez, what a dashing fellow!
With his flock of goslings, to the riverside they go, Hey!
He thinks they are his oxen, so he whistles at them, Hey!

God Bless America Tour 2004
San Diego

The Composer is waltzing with Kim to the Santana song "Oye Como Va," but the song is in five and he's waltzing in three and everyone on the boat—a moonlight cruise through Mission Bay—is staring at them. Salsa-dancing couples stop mid-sashay to make way for The Composer, who is dragging Kim in a forward line that is more tango than waltz. His face is turned away from hers and he is doing the velociraptor—that smile, all jawline and teeth, made unconvincing by the terror in his eyes. I watch the members of the live salsa band as they watch The Composer tango-waltz through the boat's cabin. After the song is done the salsa musicians announce a break and flee the stage, but not before I notice a band member with a laptop computer that is hooked up to the speakers, and I wonder if the live salsa band is actually live.

The next day I decide to get as far away from The Composer and the others as possible. I pack a plastic laundry bag with my journal, a newspaper, a bath towel, and a complimentary hotel bagel and march down to an isolated spot on Mission Beach, where I spend the entire day alone, staring into the Pacific, watching birds play in the surf.

There are so many of them, diverse in colors and sizes, a whole

Bird World flocking and dancing on the sand. There are large birds that nosedive deep into the water and explode out a few minutes later with fish wriggling in their beaks, their wings spraying sea foam as they ascend into the hazy yellow sky. There are elegant long-necked birds and birds with pencil-thin beaks. There are tiny birds that move in groups, leapfrogging over one another down the shoreline, picking at the sand for tiny scraps. There are boastful seagulls flapping up a ruckus.

One small seagull finds a clam and pretends like it's nothing so the other birds won't fight him for it. He waits for them to walk away, nonchalantly scratching his feathers with his beak. But as soon as their backs are turned he breaks open the clam and strips it of its salty meat. Even birds know the value of a good fake performance.

Another American Composer

Copland's *Appalachian Spring* was, unsurprisingly, a popular choice for classical concerts in Appalachia. We played various renditions and excerpts of it at school concerts, cloggers danced to its rhythms at heritage festivals, and church ladies hammered out the "Simple Gifts" theme on pianos and mountain dulcimers. Copland was perhaps the only American composer who classical music snobs and country bumpkins loved in equal measure. His compositions were held up as the paradigm of American classical music: Complex enough to be educational and aspirational, simple enough to hum along to, popular and catchy enough to be used in a beef commercial. (Sometimes you imagine that his "Hoedown" belches out of the

RV's exhaust pipe as you travel around America.) Copland's music
was beef all right, plus potatoes and apple pie. A real crowd-pleaser.
What could be more patriotic? More heartland America? More
classical-music-meets-Appalachian-high-school-gymnasium?

In a college music history course, you'll learn that Copland
hadn't been thinking of Appalachia when he composed *Appalachian
Spring*. He had been composing a ballet for world-renowned dancer
and choreographer Martha Graham and titled the piece *Ballet for
Martha*, until Martha herself suggested the title *Appalachian Spring*
shortly before its premiere. (She was inspired by a poem about a
bubbling mountain water spring, not the season.) For years afterward, Copland was amused when people told him that they heard
the beauty of Appalachia in his music. Like The Composer's song
titles—"Atlantic Sunrise," "Starlight of Acadia," "Ocean's Cliff"—
people thought the music had been composed to fit a specific geographical inspiration, when in fact the music was composed first,
the geographical title an afterthought. The titles of The Composer's compositions, you come to realize, share the same marketing
strategy as flavors of herbal tea: Soothing; Energizing; Sleepytime;
Tummy Tamer. Sometimes the customer just wants to be told
what to feel.

Even so, you cannot listen to Copland's music without thinking
it *does* articulate something real and true about small-town America,
something that expresses cultural complexity in a musical language
that is more precise and accurate than the spoken word. And you'll
learn that Aaron Copland—whom you'd always assumed was born
on some ranch in Kansas—was born in Brooklyn. He was Jewish,
an outspoken Communist, and gay. He was hounded for years by
McCarthy, and like most gay people of his era, was unable to openly
proclaim his sexuality. You'll marvel at his generosity, his giving

America something it would have never given him: a chance to be heard as its full, rich, complex self.

God Bless America Tour 2004

Los Angeles

"**H**ave you considered wearing an adult diaper?" your friend Nicole asks you in the ladies' room of the Skirball Center. It's your fifth trip to the bathroom in ninety minutes; three times before the concert, once during The Composer's halftime speech, and now again after the concert has finished. Nicole watches all of this with increasing worry. A year after you searched for apartments together in New York, she left for L.A. She hasn't seen you in six months and is shocked by the changes she sees in you.

Nicole was your smartest, most ambitious college friend, a hard prize to claim in the land of the hypersmart and hyperambitious. She triple-majored in philosophy, economics, and creative writing ("I had to petition the dean to take more than twenty-five credits a semester," she told you the first time you met her, in a literature class freshman year). You bonded over your unnamed workaholism and the fact that you both fought to go to Columbia—you because your parents couldn't afford the tuition, her because she had gotten into Yale and had to convince her parents to let her go to a lesser-ranked school ("Do you think I'd be working for Scorsese right now if I lived in New Haven?" is how she explained it to you). She aced her heavy course load while interning full-time for famous movie directors and running five miles a day and babysitting for extra cash and taking noncredit art classes just for fun and volunteering for third-world charities. She was the person who knew where to find the best *moules-frites* in Manhattan at three o'clock in the morning and pointed out celebrities while you chewed obliviously on your *frites*. And when Nicole returned from working for the Cannes Film Festival at the end of your junior year, she brought you back a full-length vintage ball gown in sparkly maroon fabric, a dress with such a unique cut around the breasts that it would only look good on a very specific body type, the exact body type you happen to have. "It cost nothing," she said when you stammered out some question about how you could possibly reimburse her. "I know where the deals are, even in France."

In short, Nicole is someone who you work very hard to impress (you have mentioned your PBS appearance and upcoming Carnegie Hall concert to her at least three times that day), and because of this, through no fault of her own, she is someone who you can never become as close with as you'd want. You also sometimes have a distinct suspicion that she wants to make you the subject of a documentary film about Appalachia.

But Nicole is a good friend to you, going above and beyond what most friends would. She has spent the entire day shuttling you around the hipper parts of Los Angeles, trying to nurse you back to sanity with vintage shopping and artisanal vegan meals. Nicole is a macrobiotic vegan who has never once tried tobacco or illegal drugs. She drinks rarely and only in moderation and chastely dates successful older men who bring her flowers and expect nothing from her but her company. You, on the other hand, have smoked and wined and chicken-gizzarded your way through America, and at this point in the tour your standards in men have lowered to the point where you'll sleep with anyone who isn't directly involved in the making of pennywhistle music. You work very hard to impress Nicole because, at the end of the day, she has somehow found a way to be an artist (she makes films—gorgeous, critically acclaimed films on important topics) while also living a sane, healthy life, the kind you desperately wish you could lead but somehow cannot. And now she is asking whether you might benefit from an "adult diaper," a paradoxical term if there ever was one.

"Nothing like that will help," you say curtly. You refuse to repeat the phrase *adult diaper.*

"But maybe, if your fear is peeing on stage, maybe wearing an adult diap—"

"It wouldn't help!" you all but scream at her, your sweaty hands clenching the gauze of your concert dress. "Please, let's just not talk about it. I don't want to talk about it with anyone."

Especially not you, Nicole, is what you don't say aloud. *Especially not you.*

Making a Living

A few years later you'll return to Los Angeles to visit Nicole, and you'll realize something that, in retrospect, seems so obvious you're ashamed it didn't occur to you earlier. The wear and tear of making a living—following her dreams, making her films—is evident, despite the macrobiotic diet and the exercise regimen and the healthy glow of an L.A. tan. The dishes in her kitchen are dusty, she has a heap of dirty laundry on her bedroom floor, and it dawns on you: *Things don't come easy for her either.*

And over the years you begin to see that this is true for everyone, that even the most privileged, the most talented, the most destined-for-success of your classmates are all, in one way or another, struggling. Nicole belonged to an elite group of students who possessed extreme natural abilities. You used to think of this group as the Genius Club, though they had no official designation. Their level of achievement was shocking, making the rest of the students—run-of-the-mill high school valedictorians—seem dim-witted by comparison. There was the guy you lived with sophomore year who would become a world-famous neuroscientist by the age of twenty-two. There was the knockout improv comedienne who soon joined the cast of *Saturday Night Live*. There was the future congressman who played jazz piano and had a black belt in karate, despite being blind. There was your roommate Ariel, with her internationally acclaimed cello skills, and Nora, your friend from Philadelphia who had all the top law schools fighting over her. And many others, including students in your courses who arrived via Hollywood, already famous.

But a few years after graduation, visible holes begin to appear in your notion of the Genius Club. The famous neuroscientist is caught plagiarizing articles in the *New Yorker*. The gorgeous comedienne accidentally drops the f-word on live television. Ariel's cello goes silent. Nora is laid off from her law firm. Nicole makes acclaimed films, yet she still struggles to make a living, which is not the same thing, you know now, as making money, not the same thing as winning praise, but more the rich, complex connotations of that word, *living*. Connotations that include the certainty of failure.

Any *living* that sounds too perfect to be true, any *living* that appears not to include failure, any *living* that seems easy and unsmudged by shadow, you know now, is fake.

God Bless America Tour 2004
San Francisco to Portland

The RV's air-conditioning is broken, and the cabin is sweltering with the heat from the engine and the asphalt and the sun radiating off the wide Sacramento Valley. Harriet and I are both horizontal on the foldout couch, which, until today, we didn't realize folded out. But now we've unfolded it and try to lie as still as possible in the heat. We try to nap or listen to music, but mostly we gaze listlessly upward at the hot California sky as it passes. Sometimes I glance over at Harriet and she looks like she is praying—she isn't asleep, but isn't quite in this world.

Kim is sitting up in the passenger seat alongside Patrick, who is in a particularly good mood, what my mom would call a fine fettle. Patrick's birthday was a few days ago, and, along with a cake, The Composer bought him a six-CD set of Irish music. We have been listening to "Oh Danny Boy" and its many variations (female solo vocal, pennywhistle only, fiddle only, chorus of men, chorus of women, all together now, etc., repeat, repeat, repeat) through the hot valleys between San Francisco and Redding. We listen to "Oh Danny Boy" while ascending through the shadows of the magnificent Mount Shasta. We listen to "Oh Danny Boy" in the cooler valleys of lower Oregon, where the game of shadow tag between sun and mountain and valley and river reminds me of the Shenandoah. We listen to "Oh Danny Boy" all the way to Eugene, where we stop at a Target to get supplies. And then we listen to "Oh Danny Boy" all the way to Portland, where the leaves are red and yellow, *like on the East Coast*, I think, surprised. We have finally left the summer; it won't find us for the rest of the tour. Gone are the rattle-dry valley deserts. Gone are the palm trees and the hot sandy smell of the Southwest and the hot vegetable smell of central California. The pipes, the pipes are calling. They're calling Patrick, mainly, Patrick of the broad shoulders and teary twinkle in his eye and the omnipresent God Bless America Tour jacket, the only person in our RV who is working for no pay, the only person whose love of the pennywhistle is pure and true. Patrick's love of the pennywhistle is an unwavering, undying love, and we do our best to tread lightly on it, though sometimes we fail.

True Life

New York City, Spring 2004

Your internship ends at the company that is not the *New York Times*. You are still hoping to find a permanent job or at least a paid internship that has something to do with the Middle East or the two bloody wars your country is in the process of losing. But you cannot find anything. So you sign the contract to go on the God Bless America Tour, thinking that, among other things, the tour will be a way for you to earn enough money to ship yourself off to Baghdad or Beirut or Jerusalem or Cairo to work as a freelance reporter.

A few months before the tour starts, a college friend calls you out of the blue to offer you a well-paid temporary research job at MTV. You don't even need to interview, you just show up. For the first time since you moved to New York, you experience what it's like to be given a job that you aren't even remotely qualified for, because you know the right person, because you went to the right college. You know nothing about working in television, and less than nothing about MTV. The channel wasn't available in your town growing up; the family that owned the local cable company had banned it, citing its bad influence on the youth. Some kids with satellite dishes were able to get MTV, but the network didn't have the cultural influence on teenagers in your rural town as it did in other places. The teenagers in your town overwhelmingly preferred country music.

But now you work at MTV, for a show called *True Life*. You are given a desk beside a wall of TV screens where MTV's top ten videos play on an endless loop. As you work, Britney Spears struts behind you in stewardess lingerie, serving up "Toxic" again and again.

Your first assignment, your new boss tells you, is to find young teenage girls who are pregnant and interested in appearing on what is beginning to be called "reality television." You have no idea that the research you are about to begin is MTV's toe-dip into what will become not only a *True Life* special, but also an entire series called *Teen Mom*. No one knows this, not even the MTV executives, for no one has yet realized the potential for profit in the desperation of poor pregnant teenage girls. All MTV has done so far is hire a temporary researcher to see whether such a show would be possible, and if so, what it might be like. And that temporary researcher is you.

The casting call goes up on the MTV website, and your inbox fills with emails from pregnant teenage girls around America. They write from midwestern suburbs, from coastal cities, from poor urban neighborhoods just a few miles from where you sit in MTV's headquarters in Times Square. They write from the Appalachian South, in a grammar you recognize. You write back to some of them, ask them to tell you more. And they respond with stories about their lives, big and small. They write about being kicked off their sports teams for being pregnant, about boyfriends who are committed to them, about boyfriends who have already left. They write about failed birth control, religious views against abortion, their shame and excitement and uncertainty about being pregnant. They write about prom, volleyball, their failed algebra course, their dreams of college. They send you photos of themselves in what you will come to recognize as the universal pose of the American teenage girl: half-sassy, half-pleading.

And you can't help but think of yourself at their age: 14, 16, 18. Of your terrible choice in a high school boyfriend: Fernando, who called you stupid and cheated on you. And yet, as you read the stories of pregnant girls all over America, you remember that Fernando had been your only emissary from a different world, the elite Northeast. And you recognize in the pregnant girls' stories something in your own—the utter dependence on a high school boyfriend. You realize that if you had not slept with Fernando in high school, he would not have introduced you to the idea of a life in New York City, which means you wouldn't have applied to Columbia, and you would not now be sitting at your own desk at MTV, Times Square, New York City, America, the World, the Universe.

When you were a sophomore in high school, an older girl who already had her driver's license drove you to the county health department, which, unlike so many other places in America, offered free birth control to underage girls without parental notification. The health department nurses knew your parents, knew everyone's parents, knew that gossip is gold in a small town with more churches than stoplights. And yet, to your knowledge, they never revealed the names of the underage girls seeking their clandestine services. The entire visit, including the mandatory precounseling and pelvic exam, took less than an hour and you left the clinic with a year's supply of pills that didn't cost you a cent.

It's magical to think about it now, how an hour in a dingy, three-room clinic determined the course of your life. But you didn't feel any magic at the time. What you felt was terrified. What if the pills didn't work? For the nurses—big-bosomed Southern women who called you "Honey" and told you to relax while they inserted a speculum into your vagina, women who gave birth control and STD tests, confidentially, to hundreds of underage girls in your small town so that you could all have a fighting chance—these women had been very clear on this point: Birth control pills could fail. Condoms could fail. It could all fail. And then *you* would fail. Everything— your years of hard work, the top grades, the good test scores, the violin concerts—everything would be fucked. *You* would be fucked. Doomed. There would be no college and no big city and no *making a living.* (No one ever mentioned abortion, perhaps because they were ideologically opposed to it, or perhaps because the money and transportation and logistical planning needed to travel hundreds of miles to the nearest abortion clinic, all without letting the adults in your life know, seemed impossible, probably was impossible.) You had already thought about it and decided that if you were to find yourself pregnant, you would climb the nearest mountain and jump off one of its many gorgeous cliffs. No reason for suicide seemed more compelling, no reason was more black-and-white, case-closed, than pregnancy. The ultimate curse of *life in the body* would be accidentally getting someone else's life literally inside your body.

But unlike many of the girls you grew up with, whose luck was worse, you never found yourself pregnant, so you were granted your life. And you are *living* it now at MTV, speaking on the phone with less-lucky girls all over America. These calls go on for hours. They tell you about their preeclampsia, their fear of the pain of labor, the logistics of renting a tub for water birth. They tell you about their tattoos, their favorite outfits, the new haircut they want to get. They tell you about their towns, how much they want to get out of them, how their parents are driving them nuts, how they envy you because you live in New York City and work at MTV. They tell you they want to become actresses, musicians, doctors, veterinarians. They tell you about their boyfriends' jobs, how sweet the boyfriend is, how terrible he is, or, most often, how the boyfriend's behavior, whether bad or good, has become overshadowed by the bigger picture that is taking shape in their bellies and their minds, the realization that there is (fuck!) another person growing inside of them, a person who will be here soon. The sudden, inescapable realness of that.

And so you begin to draft a report, a list of profiles of ten or so girls out of the hundreds of responses you've received. You choose the girls carefully, based on how interesting they are. The most interesting girls, to you, are the ones who have their shit together. The ones who had it all—grades, talent, ambition—but decided not to throw themselves over a cliff when they found themselves pregnant, instead resolving to work even harder. You choose the ones who, despite incredible odds of pregnancy and poverty and chaos, are taking AP courses and applying for college, the ones who run for student government while visibly pregnant, the ones who have already researched which colleges offer housing for families. The ones who are smart and capable and well-spoken and mature. The ones who will probably "make it." You find the determination of these girls nothing short of amazing, their will to live in a country that wants to shame them and shove them out of sight or off a cliff to be nothing short of miraculous.

You bring your list of profiles to your boss, who looks them over. You meet with MTV executives. And everyone tells you the same thing: Can't you find girls who are more . . . interesting?

At first you don't know what they mean. But these girls *are* interesting, you say. They are not letting their pregnancies ruin their lives! They are facing tremendous obstacles head-on! They are trying to disprove that whole "biology is destiny" thing! They are capable and mature and it will be thrilling to watch them as they work hard, harder than anyone else their age, to achieve their dreams!

We want girls with more "conflict," is how the executives put it, but what you soon realize is that they want girls who are the most naïve and the least self-aware. Girls whose personalities are so bombastic and unpredictable that they are likely dealing with undiagnosed mental illnesses. Girls whose lives are disasters. So you go back to your inbox and look for the most brazen portraits and the worst grammar. And you type up a new report.

Your new report is a list of caricatures, each profile accompanied by a sassy-pleading portrait. It is a list of stereotypes about young women in America. Here is the New Jersey slut. Here's the once-wholesome Iowa gal with a heart full of gold and a belly full of sin. Here's the trailer trash, the ghetto queen, the princess. Here is the beauty queen and here is the party girl. Here is the aspiring model and here is the aspiring porn star. Here is the Madonna and here is the whore.

This list of girls is not what you consider True Life. It is not an accurate or complete list. You tell yourself it doesn't matter anyway: Your research is preliminary, the production shoot is months away, and none of the girls you interviewed will actually appear on MTV. And yet, you feel that your final list of girl caricatures *does* matter, for it is a testament to a certain cultural desire to make American women, yourself included, seem simple, stupid, slutty. You know this desire well, for you spent your own teenage years swatting it away with a violin.

You are not yet sure how you could, in the face of pressure from a massive corporate television empire, write a different list of girls, not sure how you could shape the world in a way that might mean such a list is never again written. You turn in your list of girl caricatures and the executives praise you for it. You get a hearty paycheck. And a few days after you turn in the list you leave MTV to go on tour with The Composer, in search of your own dreams, your own America.

God Bless America Tour 2004
Portland to Seattle

Mount St. Helens and its surrounding area have been evacuated; the volcano is shooting a plume of steam and ash nine thousand feet into the sky. Ash spits onto the RV's windshield like smoke-colored snow.

Kim eyes you over the cover of her *Left Behind* book and you eye her back over your copy of *Reading Lolita in Tehran*. Every once in a while you pause to copy a quote from the book into your journal in different color Sharpies, as if you are in Azar Nafisi's forbidden literature class and taking notes:

In green: Curiosity is insubordination in its purest form.
—Vladimir Nabokov

In blue: The highest form of morality is not to feel at home in one's home.

—Theodor Adorno

In red: A good novel makes a space that is seemingly comfortable suddenly uncomfortable.

—Azar Nafisi

"What is that book about?" Kim asks, startling you. She is looking at the book's cover, which has a photograph of two Iranian women. Their heads are bent downward, as if they are reading a book together, and their black chadors are draped in such a way that the two heads seem to be of one body.

There is something alarming in Kim's tone, an undercurrent of sarcasm, perhaps, or accusation. You feel the need to defend the book, and the irony of doing so—defending a book that is about defending books—is not lost on you. You try to explain the book's premise as innocuously as possible: It's a nonfiction book about a women's book club in Iran. The women are oppressed by their families and the society in which they live, but they are able to come to a deeper understanding of this oppression and the possibilities for liberation by reading works of banned Western literature. You say something like this. But this is not the answer Kim is seeking.

What she really wants to talk about is something else, something more local, more immediate. What she really wants is to have the angry conversation that so many Americans are having these days, at their dinner tables, at their watercoolers, at their church picnics and family reunions. Even before it starts, you know what conversation this is, and that the chances of it going well are slim.

"Tell me something," she says. "Why does their religion say it's okay to kill us?"

Tell me something, Kim. Are you not reading a Left Behind *book that fantasizes about the day when all non-Christians will suffer tortuous, Book of Revelations–prophesied deaths while you and all the other Christians are raptured up to heaven where, what? Do you get seventy virgins as well?*

But you don't say that. Because you're scared. But what are you afraid of? You do not, like Azar Nafisi, live in postrevolution Iran. You do not live in mortal terror of the Ayatollah or the Secret Police. At best, you fear jeopardizing your job, but if you're being honest, what you really fear is awkwardness. You fear that Kim will become angry with you. You fear that she won't like you.

So you say something meant to be conciliatory.

"I think acts of terrorism have more to do with politics than religion," you say, cautiously. "But I agree with you that the terrorists themselves might have religious motives. Like the 9/11 hijackers probably thought they were doing something good for God's sake."

"But Muslims don't believe in God," she says.

"Of course they do," you say, shocked by this, though you know you shouldn't be. "See, that's actually kind of an offensive thing to say. 'Allah' is just the Arabic word for God. Most Muslims are really good, religious people, like religious Christians. The Quran actually contains a lot of the same stories as the Bible—"

"He's not God!" she yells, furious. "Allah is not God! He's just not!"

She throws down her book and stomps to the back of the RV, slamming the door of The Composer's room behind her.

A few hours later, when you are parked beside the PBS station in Portland, you try to reconcile with her. You don't know why you do this, other than you just want your own small world to be peaceful and comfortable. No need for the Iraq War to expand into the RV.

"Hey, uh, Kim?" you begin in your most apologetic tone. "I wasn't trying to say Allah was God . . ."

You think that somehow this statement coming out of your mouth is okay because what you're really trying to say is that you didn't mean to disrespect her Christianity, even though you don't feel like you have. But she interrupts you midapology.

"I *hope* not," she says curtly. And she turns on her heels and walks away again.

By this point you are in a rage. You are about to blow your top, explode, shoot ash, annihilate. And not only because you think Kim's views are ignorant and bigoted, but because you feel she's not even playing by the rules of her own game. You were trying to do the "Christian" thing here, you think, extend the olive branch, and she is setting the branch on fire.

You sit on a park bench beside the public television station in one of the most liberal cities in America. You know it is politically incorrect to hate someone. You know it goes against your polite secular humanist principles to hate another human being. ("Never say hate," your parents said when you were growing up. "You can never hate anyone," said the nice Wiccan lesbian vegetarian Sunday school teachers at the Unitarian Universalist Church your family attended. Enlightened liberal progressive secular humanists are free, to think or do or feel anything. Except for hate.)

But your hand shakes as you scribble Kim's words into your journal.

Like most people who find themselves in a blind rage, what you really feel, beneath the anger, is helplessness. Americans, you now realize, are no better at sniffing out bullshit propaganda about weapons of

mass destruction than they are at detecting bullshit musical performances. The war you protested has exploded into daily mass killings.
Hometown pals are losing their limbs and their minds and their lives.
And if the polls are correct, the president who started it all (Why? For
what?) is about to be reelected because people like Kim think all Muslims want to kill her. She is no better, you think, than the Egyptians
who said to your face that September 11th was cause for celebration,
that all Americans deserve to die for supporting military dictatorships
and oil kingdoms. But unlike those Egyptians, whom you never got to
know well, Kim is a visible and precise target for your rage. She's worse
than Bush, you think, because he wouldn't have been elected if not for
Kim and others like her. Ignorant America. Ugly America.

Though you don't realize it at the time, you are holding Kim—a
nice woman and talented musician who, despite not liking you, has
done plenty of nice things for you on tour—personally responsible
for the Iraq War.

No, it's worse than that. You are holding Kim responsible for
American indifference to the war, and the effect that indifference has
had on *you, personally*. For your failure to get any job in which you
could play a small role in helping bridge the deepening waters of mis-
understanding between America and the Middle East. For the way
that this failure, compounded on top of other failures, has literally
driven you crazy, to the point where you can no longer tell whether
or not your body has to pee, no longer tell what is real and what is
fake. You think you hate Kim, but what you really hate is the fact
that in the middle of two catastrophic wars, it is easier to hold a job
fake-fiddling, playing calming music for Americans while Baghdad
burns, than it is to get a job reporting from the middle of the blaze.

(Years later, in a New York City graduate-level writing class full
of Ivy Leaguers whose politics and sensibilities are the exact oppo-

site of Kim's, you will spend months writing about the Middle East.
Then, one week, you will turn in a piece about being a fake violinist
in America and everyone will say, *This*, oh *this*! *This* is so much more
interesting! *This* is what we want to read about!)

After your fight, you and Kim never again share more than a few
words. Unlike the women in *Reading Lolita in Tehran*, you and Kim
have no brilliant professor to save you, no one who encourages you
to see things from the other person's point of view. You don't share
an experience of reading a great work of literature together and
then come to a better understanding of the anger you feel toward
the political situation in your country. You don't come to respect
each other's different religious beliefs. You don't do anything except
become silent and hostile toward each other. Even your shared love
of music cannot save you.

And as for you—the person who once thought she'd be a good
war correspondent, the person who now can't stand on stage playing her violin without thinking she's going to pee on herself and
die—you blindly copy quotations with your colored Sharpie pens
while the earth rumbles and the sky rains ash. You do not question why you're doing so. You do not interrogate your own anger to
see whether it is the righteous kind born of injustice or the selfish
kind born of personal failure. You do not wander past the pride-
ful boundaries of intellectual detachment to notice what the words
might imply for you, personally:

In purple: Whoever fights monsters should see to it that in the
process he does not become a monster.

—Friedrich Nietzsche

PART IV
The Sound

We in ancient countries have our past—we obsess over the past. They, the Americans, have a dream: they feel nostalgia about the promise of the future.

—Azar Nafisi, *Reading Lolita in Tehran*

and all the children,
all of them,
waded into the music
as if it were water

—David Lee Garrison, "Bach in the DC Subway"

West Virginia
1989

All of the children in your elementary school assemble in the cafeteria, which is also the gym, which also has a small stage. It is Christmastime, and there is a Christmas star hanging above you, and you will perform "Twinkle, Twinkle, Little Star," which happens to be the only song you know how to play. This was all your idea, inserting a violin solo into the school Christmas pageant, and your teachers, who know you well enough to know that once you want to do something you will pester them until you can do it, have said, *Oh, yes. A violin song for the Christmas pageant. How nice. Sure, you can play your violin, honey.*

You are not nervous about playing your violin in front of the whole school, but your dad is. As he tucks you into bed the night before your performance, he issues gentle warnings. He says you're doing a great job with lessons and practicing, but it's just that, well, you still kind of squeak and scratch a lot. The other kids might be mean and laugh. Kids can be cruel, he says. Uh-huh, you say. They won't laugh, you tell him.

So you stand in front of the hundreds of other kids and play "Twinkle, Twinkle, Little Star." You play each note very slowly, because you cannot yet play the violin any faster than note by tortuous note. You screech. You scratch. You sound God-awful.

Just as you expected, no one laughs. Instead there is dead silence, stillness so unusual for a gymnasium full of children that years later you will remember how deep and powerful that quiet is. You scratch out the last note and the cafeteria-gym-auditorium fills with the sound of small hands clapping. You take a bow, triumphant, but are not surprised. You expected everyone to think you were great because in your eight-year-old head, a head that has not yet learned to doubt itself or feel guilty about being too showy, a head that has not yet encountered *life in the body*, you think your ability to play "Twinkle, Twinkle, Little Star" speaks for itself. You think it's great, and so it's no surprise to you that the other kids think it's great, too.

But later you do overhear kids saying something bad about you, something very surprising. You are in the girl's bathroom after the pageant, and two older girls who you don't know are talking about you.

"Was she really playing the violin?" one girl asks.

"No way," the other girl says. "It was a tape player."

"Yeah, it was a tape player," the first girl agrees.

You are so shocked by this conversation, so angry, so determined to set the record straight, that it doesn't occur to you that this is a twisted sort of compliment—these girls thought your scratchy squeaky playing was too good to be believed. You had been warned that the kids might laugh at you; you had never considered they'd regard you as too good to be real. But many of them did. They came up to you on the playground, in the lunch line, on the school bus, and asked, "Were you *really* playing?"

Yes, you say. Yes, yes. It was real. It wasn't a tape player. Yes, I can prove it. Yes, yes, it was real, it was real, it was real. Yes, I was really playing. Yes, it was really me.

Who Is The Composer? III

What The Pirate says:
There are actually two pirates, Good Pirate and Bad Pirate, both played by The Composer. The VHS tape—a thirty-minute demo of a children's television program—opens with Good Pirate wearing a tricorn, wig, and mustache. He has three mates on his ship: a parrot, a fish, and a small purple dinosaur that appears to be Barney, but whom Good Pirate calls Diney. Diney is cradled in Good Pirate's arm, for Diney is first mate.

It is almost impossible to make out what Good Pirate says because he mumbles in an accent that can only be described as cockney meets surfer dude, though it is possible to ascertain that the phrase "great thundering pirates" is used at least seven times in thirty minutes. Good Pirate and his stuffed animals are on a ship. They have a map that grants wishes. The bird wishes to find his long-lost bird parents, so Good Pirate intones, "Oh ye map, oh ye map," and the ship sails "straight to the North Star." But not nautically, as in *the direction of* the North Star. No, the ship actually goes to outer space.

But then! The screen splits. Bad Pirate appears. Bad Pirate, played by The Composer with his hair slicked back, steals the show. He is the video's only comprehensible character, speaking in the hyper-articulated vowels stereotypically assigned to gay men. Bad Pirate's accent is consistent and convincing. Bad Pirate holds a mirror up to his face as he talks. He is surrounded by gold coins and empty wine bottles. Whenever Bad Pirate appears, the music changes from the pirated sounds of the *Titanic* soundtrack to the pirated sounds of smooth jazz.

"Tag! You're it!" says Bad Pirate to Good Pirate.

God Bless America Tour 2004
Seattle

"**F**uck The Composer!" Harriet yells.

We are a Seattle postcard: Space Needle. Pouring rain. A shared umbrella. Both of us too drunk on the beer from a grunge-deco bar to hold the umbrella properly.

"Fuck him!" she yells again. She hands me the umbrella and runs away, toward the Space Needle.

"Where are you going?" I yell after her.

"Fuck him!" she yells as she runs farther and farther away.

Harriet has never acted like this before. Before this moment, she has traveled across America while keeping her normal composure—a cheery, faith-based serenity so unshakable that at times I wonder if she is actually an eighty-year-old Midwestern church lady trapped in the body of a cover girl. We joke about The Composer on a regular basis in private. But yelling "Fuck The Composer!" and running around in the rain under the Space Needle marks a new level of dissatisfaction.

Years later, I ask her what she was so upset about and neither one of us will be able to remember the specifics. Our suspicion is that something pissed her off at the concert that night. Harriet had graduate degrees in violin performance from good conservatories, but each night, The Composer introduced her as the woman with "the biggest, most beautiful smile." Perhaps, after dozens of concerts, she was sick of smiling, sick of carrying the weight of beauty for a musical imposter who couldn't (or wouldn't) appreciate her actual talent. Or maybe it was the fact that The Composer had five boxes of apples FedExed to Seattle from Maine, and there was nowhere in the RV to stand or sit. *We've been replaced by fruit*, I can hear her saying. *Maybe he can just put those apples on stage during the concerts and we can go home.*

The next morning we leave for Boise, Idaho. Harriet enters the RV, calmly removes a box of apples from the foldout couch, and takes a seat. But something in her demeanor is changed. She has a wild look, like, *I dare you to fuck with me. I dare you to say I have the biggest, most beautiful smile. Just one more time. Just one more fucking time.*

Anger

I saw The Composer get angry once. It was a Sunday afternoon at a run-down mall in Kansas. Kim and I played like robots for hours, but for once there were no crowds of adoring fans around the CD table. The Composer sat forlornly at the customerless sales table, gazing for hours into the storefront of a Sears, where shoppers examined lawn tractors. Eventually a few people approached our sales table, but they did so cautiously, as if afraid of committing to something. After all, buying music is not the same as buying a tractor. You cannot see it, touch it, examine its gears. Music is a tricky product. It's abstract, effusive, intangible. Music makes no guarantees. At the same time, music is the easiest of purchases. Do you like what you're listening to? If so, take it home and listen some more. If not, move on. But on that day our customers seemed reluctant to trust their own ears. They stood far away from the sales table and shouted questions about genre: *Is this classical music?* Sometimes The Composer said that it was. Other times he called it "instrumental music," a term brilliant for its simultaneous accuracy and evasiveness.

All of a sudden my E string exploded into shreds. I instinctively stopped playing to survey the damage and unwind the frayed end of the broken string from its peg. Before I realized what was happening, The Composer cut the power to the music and marched toward me. He was furious. He came very close to me, inches from my face. For the first time since I'd met him, he looked me directly in the eye. His face had a coldness I had never seen before. I looked down, panicked with the too-late realization that my broken string had just jeopardized our entire charade. Even the least sophisticated Kansan would know that listening to flawless violin music while watching the violinist bust an E string was a sure sign of the Milli Violini.

In a different context, a broken E string could be a sign of genius. Take Midori Goto, the fourteen-year-old violin prodigy who made world headlines in 1986 when, as she performed a solo at Tanglewood with the Boston Symphony Orchestra, she broke her E string, took another violin, broke that E string, took another violin, and continued the performance without missing a note. When the performance was over, Leonard Bernstein fell to his knees before her. The Midori story, which I read about when I was eight years old, a few months after beginning violin lessons, was a devastating revelation. For a few days after reading it, I wanted to quit the violin. The Midori story was my first encounter with the idea of prodigy, the idea that there are people in the world who can play the violin better at eight years old than most professionals can after a lifetime of practice. It was a shockingly un-American idea: No matter how hard you work, you'll never be as good as someone who was born great.

The Composer had afforded me a career in which I could skip past the Midori problem, ignore the contradiction inherent in having mediocre violin skills, yet putting "Violinist" as my profession on my tax returns. But on that day in Kansas, as I stood with my head hanging in shame, my E string dangling limp and silent, there was no Leonard Bernstein kneeling before me in awe. There was only The Composer towering above me, hissing at me in a low, hard voice: "MELISSA! Never, NEVER stop playing! NEVER!"

I wish I had said to The Composer that there was no way for any violinist, no matter how good, to prevent the occasional broken string. I wish I had said that in all of my time working for him, I had never received any explicit instructions for what to do if a string broke, that neither he nor anyone in a management position had ever acknowledged the fact that what we were doing was the Milli Violini. But I didn't say any of this. I didn't yell, "Fuck The Composer!" I didn't even roll my eyes.

What I did, instead, was apologize. Perhaps I did this because immediate apology is the default female response to male rage (survival mechanism). Perhaps I did this because The Composer was my boss and I was his employee (The Money). Perhaps I did this because I was one of many young female musicians The Composer employed, many of whom were more attractive than me, and because of this I often felt unworthy of the job (*life in the body*).

Or perhaps I apologized because I hadn't yet learned that I was capable of expressing anger. I didn't know that if I was angry it need not be confined to the quiet pages of a private journal but could be screamed aloud (Harriet running toward the Space Needle).

Not expressing anger was what made me "a very easy person to work with." I hadn't yet learned I could be so much more than that.

God Bless America Tour 2004
Minneapolis

The first thing you notice about the Mall of America is the crowd of people outside of it, taking photographs. You have seen these types of crowds before, encircling the monuments in Washington, D.C., the Statue of Liberty, the Empire State Building. You've seen these crowds gaping over the ragged rim of that monstrous hole in Lower Manhattan, the one that reminds you of the diagrams in Dante's *Inferno*, a nonmonument that you can't bring yourself to visit, though you once glimpsed its crowds through a window at Century 21, the discount women's clothing store where you bought a new black gauzy concert dress for your tour around America. Yes, you've seen these types of tourist crowds before, with their baseball caps and t-shirts and fleece pullovers and tiny backpacks and cargo pants and sneakers. But there is something different about the crowd on the sidewalk in front of the Mall of America; these pilgrims are more engaged in their series of rites. For the Mall of America is the national shrine at which it is most possible not just to see America but to *do* it, to perform its sacraments. To drink its caffeinated, carbonated blood. To inhale the national incense: french fry grease, fabric softener, the sour chemical smell of fresh ink on a sales receipt.

So you go to the least-American place you can find in the Mall of America, a restaurant in the middle of Minnesota called California Cafe, and you order the Merlot and the artisan cheese plate. But you're fooling yourself, for in the very act of biting into your hard cheddar garnished with truffle honey you are only practicing another timeworn American tradition: acting like you are French.

Later that day, after you play "Atlantic Sunrise," the penny whistle-spangled anthem that has launched a million CD sales, the song that sounds just like our national, pre-9/11 movie *Titanic*, after the eagle has flown over the Grand Canyon and The Composer has attempted to waltz with a woman in a wheelchair in front of a packed crowd of your applauding countrymen, you recross the Mississippi, a smaller, more ice-flecked river than the one you crossed a month ago in Memphis. And hours after this, after you have reentered the rolling hills where the grass is the lighter, zestier green that you now know can only be found in the East, after you have finished hanging your ragged clothes in a hotel in rural Wisconsin, you check your email and see a message from Jake, The Composer's manager:

> *I have some unfortunate news regarding the Carnegie Hall show. The promoter has decided to cancel the show as of today . . . Feel free to give me a call if you have any questions.*

But you will not "feel free to call with any questions," because you know that asking questions is the surest route in America to getting your ass fired. You will certainly not ask the most important ones: Hadn't Jake mentioned, a few months ago, that the concert had sold out? Was the concert canceled because the promoter figured out the performance wouldn't be live? And if so, who spilled the beans? Was the integrity of our nation's most prestigious concert stage saved, at least for this moment, by a tall Russian violinist who once studied at Moscow Conservatory?

Colder Than Russia

Yevgeny loved listening to techno and electronica music on our way to gigs. Moby was at the top of the charts in those early years of the millennium. We listened to "Go" in a January blizzard while driving to a convention center in Ocean City, Maryland, where we hawked The Composer's CDs to stunned-looking women wandering desolate aisles of discounted Christmas wares. We ate chicken strips in Wilkes-Barre, Pennsylvania, on a summer night and drove home smoking cigarettes while "Porcelain" rolled over us like a club drug. The places blend together in my memory, but the downbeat-laden dance club soundtrack is the same: A snow-logged New England town that had a Hawaiian restaurant with a room-size replica of a magma-shooting volcano. A steakhouse in Oklahoma City with a menu that promised a free meal to anyone who could eat five pounds of steak in one sitting.

A lakeside bar in Cleveland where I drank too much of something called "Christmas Ale" and vomited fried cod in our rental car. A cosmetics counter in a Connecticut mall where Yevgeny watched as I spritzed myself with a pink-bottled vanilla perfume. My first glimpse of Niagara Falls, misting across the street from our craft fair tent.

I think Yevgeny admired the way that techno sampled authentic music and looped it into endless repetition—a perfect synthesis of the real and the artificial. It's been many years since I've seen him, but the right music brings him back to me. Once, when we were on a gig—maybe in Cleveland, or Miami, or Connecticut—Yevgeny told me about the time he went on tour with The Composer and Kim, a few years before the God Bless America Tour. The three of them visited nearly every Barnes and Noble in the country, performing The Composer's latest CD beside stacks of best sellers, competing against the roar of espresso machines. But instead of a modern RV, they drove an older model that was more like a trailer attached to a pickup truck. The Composer and Kim sat in the front cab while Yevgeny curled up in the trailer's loft bed. The trailer didn't have working heat. And during one long night's drive through Montana, Yevgeny thought he was going to freeze to death.

I laughed. A Russian emigrating for a better life only to freeze to death in America. How Russian!

"I know it's funny," he said. "But I thought I was going to die. It was colder than Russia. Colder than I've ever been. That's when I knew he didn't care about me. If I had died, he would have been like 'Well, we will have to fly another violinist to Montana.'"

I listened to this sympathetically. At that point in his life, Yevgeny was still in a precarious situation, immigration-wise. He had visa paperwork that had to be filled out. He had an accent. He didn't have family or money to help if things went south. The Composer could have had him deported. What happened to Yevgeny could never happen to me. People—American citizens—would notice if I froze to death in the back of a trailer.

But years later I realized that Yevgeny hadn't told me about nearly dying in Montana because he wanted my sympathy. He was trying to warn me, to tell me to be careful on the God Bless America Tour. I didn't freeze to death, but I did suffer a constant fear—delusional, I had assumed—that I was in mortal danger.

I considered this further. Perhaps the danger had not been imaginary. Patrick, who had never driven an RV, was sometimes assigned to drive fourteen-hour stretches at a time. At night, he drank Irish whiskeys until he stumbled back to his room, only to rise the next morning and set out on the perilous road in an RV that was becoming more dilapidated with each mile. The Composer duct-taped the dangling side mirrors, ignored our complaints when the air-conditioning broke in the middle of the sweltering California desert. There were dozens of close calls involving narrow lanes and swerving tractor trailers. And there were other types of close calls, nights when Harriet and I escorted each other through the corridors of cut-rate motels, wary of the men who eyed us in the parking lot, men who followed us as we made our way to the laundry room, fitness center, snack machine. While I survived the tour physically intact, I lost my grip on reality. And no one really noticed until I returned from the tour and collapsed on the floor of my parents' basement.

Yevgeny was able to state—simply and without fanfare—that The Composer had almost killed him. It would take me years of drafting and revising this book to say essentially the same thing.

Praeludium and Allegro

Virginia, 1998

Your last solo concert takes place in a similar setting to your first: a Christmas concert in an Appalachian gymnasium packed with the entire student body. But this time you are a senior in high school, keenly aware of the other students. They sit on the bleachers and in metal folding chairs. The girls pull out notebook paper and write notes to one another, and the boys spit sunflower seeds or chewed tobacco into plastic Mountain Dew bottles. The sleepy-eyed teachers stand at the ends of the bleachers, arms folded, watching for troublemakers. The PE teacher—wearing shorts even in the dead of winter—gazes longingly at the basketball hoop, his silver whistle resting silently on his broad chest.

You stand at the back door of the gym. Rhinestone poinsettia hair clips rein your wild black hair; your sleeveless, gauzy black dress grazes the freshly polished wood of the basketball court. You shift your violin from hand to hand as you wipe your sweaty palms on your dress.

The principal walks to the front of the gym and begins the concert by telling everyone to sit still and shut up. The band wheezes a half-hearted Christmas carol. A group of boys in the bleachers kick one another. The Spanish teacher looks up from her grading stack and shoots them a look.

You are going to perform Fritz Kreisler's "Praeludium and Allegro in the Style of Pugnani," the piece another violinist once chose as the best possible music to entertain Truman, Churchill, and Stalin at Potsdam. It's *that* kind of piece. The minute you heard Nadja Salerno-Sonnenberg's unparalleled recording of it, when you were eleven, you knew you had to learn to play it. It took you six years to untangle, note by note, measure by measure. It is one of the flashiest, most attention-grabbing, most look-at-me pieces ever written for the violin—the kind of piece that movie directors choose when they want to show someone is a violin prodigy (the violinists in *Prince of Tides* and *Sea of Love* play it). The piece garners a specific type of audience response, one that could be called "The Holy Shit"—that deep silence that fills a room after a musician does something that seems physically impossible and therefore magical. That's what you are going for here; you are aiming for The Holy Shit.

Years after this performance, your mom will tell you what one of the high school teachers said to her about this concert: "I was afraid they were going to laugh at her. You know how kids are."

You have learned a lot about "how kids are" since your first concert, nine years earlier, when you stood in a different school gymnasium in a different part of Appalachia and played "Twinkle, Twinkle, Little Star." Since then you have begun to learn what it is like to live *life in the body*. What it's like to despair so much at the prospect of *life in the body* that you almost chose to end that life. "Jessica has big lips," says a boy in your seventh-grade prealgebra class. "That means she gives good blow jobs." *Life in the body* means that no physical part of you—not even the lips that you have no choice but to bring with you into prealgebra class—is left unseen, unremarked upon, uncalculated for sexual potential. By ninth grade, girls lived the quiet, starving denial of *life in the body* while boys scribbled a simple acronym on the chalkboards, the lockers, the desks—an acronym all the students knew the meaning of, but the teachers did not: GOYK. The boys held up pieces of notebook paper reading: GOYK! You walked into your tenth-grade

chemistry classroom and there it was on the chalkboard: GOYK!
"Why don't you just GOYK?" the boys asked the girls in the high
school hallways. GOYK! read the inscription on the door to the
girl's bathroom, the backs of the school bus seats, the undersides
of the desks. GOYK was spelled out in garlic powder on the windshield of your dad's old Nissan, which he let you drive to a party one
night. (The garlic was a nod to you being Italian American. Boys
call you "the dark one," half *Star Wars* joke, half ethnic slur. And
when you rinse off the garlic at a car wash before returning home,
it drains into the heating vents leaving the Nissan to smell like a
zesty Italian restaurant forevermore, a metaphor for the impossi-
bility of escaping *life in the body*, even in your own car.) GOYK! they
wrote in your yearbook. "GOYK!" they laughed as they slapped
one another's backs.

GOYK. Get. On. Your. Knees. (And suck my dick.)

You've learned a lot about kids laughing at one another, all right,
more than you could have ever imagined when you were eight years
old and playing "Twinkle, Twinkle, Little Star." And you've learned
how to avoid it, have developed dozens, maybe hundreds of strate-
gies over the years. You wear the right socks. You curl your hair. You
shave your legs, your underarms, your bikini line. You hide pimples
under pressed powder. You beg your parents for certain dresses, certain skirts, certain shoes that you see in the catalogs for teenage girls
that arrive in your rural mailbox. You exercise for hours each day
in an attempt to be as skinny as possible. You sunbathe. You track
your period so it doesn't end up on the back of your shorts. You learn
how to laugh when the boys say GOYK so they think you're cool
and down with it and on their side and leave you alone. You learn
how to flirt and be a little quieter than you are. You learn how to
surround yourself with other girls, to run in a pack. You date pop-

ular boys, even though you can tell they don't like you very much, even though they routinely cheat on you, because in the cold calculus of high school social dynamics, dating popular boys elevates you beyond a status you could achieve for yourself, and not just in the eyes of your classmates, but in the eyes of some of your teachers, too. You catch the quick but unmistakable flashes of appreciation on their adult faces when they see you standing in the ambient light that radiates off of the six foot two inch rock-solid figure of future-Docker's-khakis-model Fernando, some ancient, nostalgic longing for the magnificent teenage sex they imagine you're having. And because you have not yet developed feelings toward yourself (other than negative feelings about your body), you see yourself only as a reflection of what other people think of you.

Except, that is, for the one public situation where you are able to be a full human being. Even throughout the brutal years of middle and high school, you have been able to keep this one idea intact: The other kids won't laugh at you when you're playing the violin. They just won't.

You take your place at the front of the gymnasium and adjust your music stand. You don't feel nervous. You feel pumped, amped-up. Years later you'll marvel at the small yet profound difference between adrenaline-fueled focus and adrenaline-fueled panic. Your accompanist—the eccentric town piano teacher who generously volunteers her virtuosic skills whenever you need them—takes her seat at the school's piano that has been rolled into the gym from the sports equipment closet. You plant your left foot so your toes align with the scroll of your violin. You lift your violin to your chin and nestle the chinrest button into the soft flesh of your neck. You align the five fingers of your right hand into the correct bow position—

thumb curved under like a claw, forefinger slightly jutting out, middle and ring fingers arched gently, the pinkie perched on top. You take one sharp breath and begin.

The praeludium's slow tempo makes it seem easy to play. The piece starts off in the lower realm of the violin, where any beginner can hit the notes. But then, slowly, it marches upward, toward the highest notes, the nose-picking section. If the violinist loses focus, the piece becomes a shrieking mess. And yet, the greatest challenge of the praeludium is not the high-pitched notes. It is the violinist's knowledge that the allegro—The Holy Shit Allegro—is coming up next.

When you reach the last note of the praeludium you barely pause. You don't want to give anyone the chance to clap between movements, but most of all you don't want to have time to think about what you're going to do next. You take another sharp breath, you stop thinking, stop being. You are just doing:

Already two lines deep because it's that damn fast. So fast the fingers can't be seen. They blur in the silver horizon above the left hand. Arpeggios. Waves of notes. Hundreds more coming up, already past. Double-stops: Two notes, three notes, four crashing notes at a time and the bow goes from down up down to da-down-da-down-up-up da-lift-da up, lift, lift, plant da-down. Bow hairs breaking under the strain. And now here is The Holy Shit. The piano accompaniment drops out and plays one deep rumbling. Your fingers fly up the neck of your violin. You dangle on the highest note like a mountain climber clinging to the summit by a fingertip. It is never about conquering the mountain. It is always about conquering the fear of the fall. Six years of practicing these sixteenth notes one note at

*a time at 60 beats per minute. Then 90. Then 125. Now at 168.
In the background, beyond the notes, there is the silence. The deep,
profound silence of an audience that has stopped moving. There is
nothing on earth like it. A moment—this moment—is no longer
life in the body. You are outside the body. No one, not even you, is
thinking about your body. Now the descent down the violin's fingerboard, a knotted downward ladder, a cat's cradle of notes, some
repeated, some not. A countermelody: it sounds like two entirely
different songs, on two different violins, coming out of one. Sweeping
arpeggios. Bow hairs breaking from both ends with puffs of rosin
smoke. Last line: Adagio. Slow down. As if to say, there you have
it, ta-da, hold the last note all the way to the frog, vibrato, Holy
Shit, done.*

It was far from the best performance of "Praeludium and Allegro"
that the world has ever heard. There were mistakes. I missed notes
in the double-stops, flubbed several arpeggios. I doubt I maintained
a pace of 168 beats per minute. But it was the best violin performance of my life, the best that my body and my violin would ever
allow me to produce. And everything about it—from the technical
aspects like the power needed for the praeludium, to the mental
concentration required for the allegro, to the eventual transforma-
tion of deep silence to a thunderous standing ovation that lasted
even longer than I expected (I knew they wouldn't laugh), a standing
ovation that people mentioned to me years later after I had left for
New York to become a "professional violinist"—everything about
the performance was real.

God Bless America Tour 2004

Chicago

A few days after the Carnegie Hall concert is canceled, the Ensemble performs in front of the largest audience yet on the God Bless America Tour. Nearly five hundred people wearing semi-formal attire arrive at a glittering concert hall in Chicago. When the ushers open the auditorium's grand doors, the crowd enters with hushed reverence, checking their tickets and finding their places in the dizzying rows of red plush velvet seats. The large stage is almost bare; there are three microphone stands and an electric keyboard. A large mustachioed man wearing an official God Bless America Tour 2004 jacket does crowd control, answering questions, selling CDs, manning the film projectors, a teary twinkle in his eye.

Enter The Composer stage left, bouncing toward the keyboard with childlike exuberance, waving and beaming at the cheering audience. He wears a blue suit jacket with black pants and black running sneakers. Two violinists and a flutist follow him onto the stage. The Composer presses the Play button on a portable Sony CD player he bought at a Walmart back in Philadelphia for $14.95.

One of the violinists—the short girl with glittering rhinestone barrettes in her long dark hair, the one who is younger than the other musicians—this violinist flees the stage while The Composer talks to the audience about The Hollywood Celebrity. She returns a few minutes later, just as The Composer tells the audience he is praying for them to keep safe, as if they are in mortal peril, as if right after the concert the audience will leave their seats, exit the glittering concert hall, and storm the beaches of Normandy. If anyone in the audience turns to the person beside him to whisper, "Well, gee, guess that one violinist gal had to pee!" they are wrong. She does not have to pee, which she knows even as she sprints to the bathroom.

Her brain is scrambled. She will die (but not before peeing herself), her legs breaking, her mouth vomiting blood. Will she knock out her teeth when she faints headfirst onto the stage? Or will she fall backward and smash the back of her skull? Will the force of her body hitting the floor cause the stage lights to loosen from the rafters and fall down on top of her, electrocuting her and setting her on fire? Or will her ribs pop loose from her rib cage while her lungs slowly deflate? And at what point in this process will she stop smiling? Will her violin be crushed under the weight of her falling corpse, or will it survive intact? Will her parents donate it to some ambitious youngster in Appalachia? Some kid who loves the sound of the violin and thinks if they practice—very hard, every day—they can become anything they want to be, because hell, this is America?

Somewhere in the back of her disaster brain—the brain that is firing the wrong signals, that tells her she is not running from a bear but already being devoured by it—she is learning something important. And the lesson is this: There is something in the world far more terrifying than humiliation or failure or death. And it is just like FDR said: Fear itself. And if she doesn't murder the bastard, this archvillain called Fear, she's going to be toast for real. She doesn't yet have a plan for vanquishing him. She has yet to learn about psychiatric remedies. She doesn't yet know why Fear has chosen this moment in her life to make his sudden entrance, licking his chops. For the early twenties, a particularly cruel age to be struck down by fear, is a stage in life when tremendous bravery is required of a woman—the bravery to discover what she wants, what she cannot abide, what she needs to make a living and be among the living.

But she knows this: A million times more than any other emotion or experience, fear has the strength and ability to mangle her into something different from what she truly is, something phony and fake and cowardly. And now, surprised and twisted and disoriented and broken as she is by fear's sudden arrival, she realizes that she needs to fight it, fight for her life.

God Bless America Tour 2004
Cincinnati to Kent

The volunteers at the Cincinnati PBS station meet our RV at the loading dock and beg us to hurry as fast as we can. There was a drive-by shooting of the station the week before, they say. It's not safe for us to be out here with the equipment and the instruments. Who does a drive-by shooting of a PBS station? I ask, hoping the answer is "Muppets." Oscar is the obvious culprit, but my money is on Burt. It's always the quiet one with obsessive hobbies.

The real answer is less exciting: "Gangs," the PBS volunteer says. "Gangs." After the concert we hightail it out of Cincinnati, leaving behind a hotel where the only thing louder than the drunken sex workers stumbling down the corridors were the cockroaches scuttling off to the side to make way, cockroaches so numerous that Harriet and I kept our hotel room light on all night to prevent cockroach parades across our sleeping faces. Good-bye, Cincinnati, we say. Good-bye and good luck.

We drive on a secondary road through rural Ohio. It is late at night. I sit up in the passenger seat with Patrick. Led Zeppelin's

"When the Levee Breaks" plays at low volume. *Got what it takes to make a mountain man leave his home.* We pass through rural town after rural town, some so dark they seem less like towns and more like hallucinations in the night. The skeletons of dark Victorians, their lightless windows like hollow eyes, watch us as we go by. The one stoplight in each town casts a green glow on an empty world. Driving through these towns at night is like driving through a memory of someone else's dream. *When the levee breaks, mama, you got to move.*

The next day, somewhere in the countryside outside of Canton, Ohio, we stop at a Blimpie sandwich shop. There is a two-dollar special going on for the meatball sub and the place is packed, the line out the door. I wait in line, too. I know everyone here, or feel like I do, like I grew up with all of them. There is the sweet-looking teenage waitress with a butterfly tattoo on the back of her neck, the potbellied truck driver with his thumb in his belt loop, the nurse's assistant in the teddy-bear–printed scrubs, the frail elderly couple leaning on each other as they look up at the sandwich menu. *These are country people,* I think. *Small-town people.* I know it is so because I was once one of them. But I don't know if I'm one of them anymore. The only reason I can recognize small-town, country people—the only reason I see them as distinct—is because I left them behind.

I can see, as the small-town people greet the Blimpie sandwich workers by name and ask about their families, that they (we?) know something that suburbanites and city dwellers don't. There is a unique wisdom of the small American community, the isolated rural hamlet, and it is this: Everyone matters. Not in some clichéd humanistic sense, but in a literal, practical sense. For in a town of a few thousand people or less, the person who makes your meatball sub at the Blimpie is the same person who raised you at the day care, will raise *your* kids at the day care, the same person who will arrive with the volunteer Rescue Squad and perform CPR on your unbreathing body, the same person who will empty your bedpan in the nursing home, the same person who will cremate your bones, bake a casserole for your funeral, auction off your worldly possessions when you are gone from this earth.

A sudden gust of wind blows through the open door of the Blimpie and a great roar comes from the sky. We, the country people, turn away from the sandwich counter, our hair blowing back, the truck driver losing his hat. There, in the field in front of the Blimpie, is Air Force One, touching down in America's most contested swing state a few days before the election. We stare and gape at the plane. But then the wind dies down and we all turn back toward the two-dollar meatball subs and the smoothie machine and the rack of potato chips. We only have a few more minutes to procure our lunches before getting back to work—at the school, the hospital, the nursing home, the funeral parlor, the fake violin tour. And then, after work is done and the kids are put to bed and the town goes silent and dark except for the green glow of the one stoplight, there will be time for dreaming.

God Bless America Tour 2004
Kent, Ohio

That night in Kent, The Composer says he wants to talk to us before the concert begins. He is concerned, *very concerned*, about our lack of smiling. Some people out there have cancer, guys!

Everything is riding on us smiling, it is life and death, and here we are, not doing it enough. (We aren't smiling, I think, because we trained for years to focus only on what music sounds like, not what it looks like, and smiling widely with a flute in the mouth or violin under the chin prevents the best sound. Smiling is no virtue to sound. It is silent. It gets in the way.) We smile and promise him we will smile.

I usually respond to The Composer's smile lectures by mocking them later with Harriet, in the privacy of a hotel room. But now, in Kent, I feel something different, something like the old me, the girl who once stormed the small-town stage and played the violin for real, the girl who once thought she could be a war correspondent, because she was brave and kept a cool head and never worried about whether or not she had to pee.

And so, when we step on the stage I smile. Like a lunatic. I smile my fake smile with an overenthusiasm that would appear insane even to the most hardcore fan. When The Composer turns to look at me so we can share smiles in the middle of the opening song, he recoils in horror. For a brief but memorable moment he stops smiling and the ever-present terror in his eyes becomes the singular, pronounced emotion on his face. Then he wrenches his stage smile back on and tries to avoid looking at me. But he can't help occasional furtive peeks. Each time he glances at me he sees me smiling back at him, but my smile is too wide, too over-the-top, too fake. I am giving him the velociraptor.

After the concert, he doesn't know what to say to me. "Wow . . . um . . . you were really smiling!" is what he says. But we both know I have beaten him at his own game, have used his own weapons against him. We both know he'll never ask me to fake smile again.

"Smile!" said the teachers in middle school, a time of life when everyone is

universally miserable. "*Don't y'all respect yourselves? Have some pride!*" "*Smile!*" *said the Denny's training video you watched in high school to become a ranch- and syrup-covered server of pancakes making less than minimum wage.* "*No one wants to get food from someone who is unhappy!*" "*Smile!*" *command the men gathered on street corners in New York City, the ones you pass at sunset on your way back from the subway or the grocery store or the laundromat.* "*You'd be a whole lot prettier with a smile on that face . . .*"

It's only then, after the hardcore fans have left and we're packing up and The Composer says, "Wow . . . um . . . you were really smiling!" that I realize, for the first time since Little Rock, Arkansas, I didn't have a panic attack during the concert. My rebellion of over-the-top fake-smiling saved me. I didn't flee the stage at halftime. I didn't think once about having to pee or my impending death. Not once.

Who Is The Composer? IV

What he says, when Harriet asks him to give his thoughts on the God Bless America Tour:

The Composer: We met a lot of really, really nice people. We had a really, really good time. It was really fun just saying, "Hi, everyone!" And meeting them. They were really nice. Weren't they nice? They were nice people. It was great! And you know sometimes, sometimes, sometimes we didn't sell CDs. So it was burgers tonight, you know what I'm saying? But at other times it was okay . . . I guess all I want to say is that it really never ends.

Harriet: That's for sure.

The Composer: All my life's a circle from sunrise to sundown.

Harriet: The circle of life? Is that what it is?

The Composer: No, that's when people eat each other and stuff.

Harriet: Oh my.

The Composer: No, this is like, a circle, a sunrise, like to give you hope . . .

Harriet: Okay.

The Composer: The circle of life is more like if you eat something like a fish, well . . .

Harriet: You poop it out and something else eats it?

The Composer: Yeah, no. This is something different. Like this is *my* circle. *Your* circle ends at the end of the tour. I'm eating you. I'm sorry. It's kind of like a bad way of saying sorry. You know, so you don't have to feel guilty? You know what I'm saying?

If It Sounds Like *Titanic*
2005

I worked for The Composer for nearly four years. In all of that time, there was only one concert in which my violin was truly audible. It did not happen in Blessed America. It happened in China.

After the God Bless America Tour ended, I hid in my parents' basement, dodging lethargic wasps that fell out of the rafters onto my foldout bed. I became skilled at Mario Bros. while worrying whether my sessions with the town psychiatrist would work if I took too many bathroom breaks. It went on like this, day after day, waking up, winning the princess from the dragon, and wondering whether I would ever be able to make it a few hours in a public setting without having a full-blown panic attack. How would I ever get a real job? The Middle East was now out of the question. I didn't even know if I could make it through the day as an office assistant, let alone a war reporter.

Then one day Jake called me to see if I could do a gig: a three-week, eight-city tour of China. *I don't care how crazy I am*, I thought. *I'm going.*

When I look back at the Ensemble's tour of China, what strikes me is how much confusion there was. There was the usual bewilderment of being in a foreign country and not speaking the language, but that wasn't enough to explain the bizarre scenarios that the Ensemble found itself in on a daily basis. For there was also the confusion of bringing a fake musical performance to a foreign country, and the confusion of being in China with The Composer—a man who did plenty of confusing things in his own country, a man who was generally confused no matter what the setting, a man who believed that everything would be okay if we all smiled—even though smiling at strangers in China can be misinterpreted (or correctly interpreted depending on your point of view) as foolishness.

I stood on the stage with The Composer and ten other musicians at the Shanghai Concert Hall—one of China's oldest and most prestigious European-style venues—a gorgeous two-tiered auditorium painted vibrant shades of blue and gold with classical archways and renowned acoustics (Yo-Yo Ma had recently performed there). The place was filled to capacity with nearly one thousand audience members. Once they were in their seats, the lights dimmed, we walked out onto the stage, and The Composer pressed the Play button on the CD player. The sounds of almost-*Titanic* filled the Chinese auditorium. The eagle flew over the Grand Canyon. We didn't have a translator on stage so The Composer didn't make any speeches or tell any stories. After the last song we took a bow and were joined on stage by a handful of teenage girls wearing yellow uniforms with red sashes. They handed us flowers and we all stood there grinning, while stern-faced Chinese officials made speeches that weren't translated. The Composer smiled his widest, most ridiculous velociraptor smile yet, the fear in his eyes more evident than ever.

The day after our Chinese debut in Shanghai, Chinese government officials canceled half of our scheduled concerts. Whether this was because The Composer's smiling was freaking out the Chinese or because the highly musically trained Chinese elite could tell that we were doing the Milli Violini, or some other reason—I did not know. But the strangest thing about having half our concerts canceled was that the concerts we *did* perform were outrageously well attended. Our popularity was a mystery to me until, during one concert, a translator told me what was being announced to the audience of four thousand people: That we, the Ensemble, were the orchestra "that played the music in the movie *Titanic*." It suddenly made sense why thousands of people had shown up to see us. And unlike in America, where such a false claim could lead to lawsuits, there didn't seem to be any immediate danger in announcing to thousands of people that we were playing *Titanic*. It was as if, after years of deceit in America (it's not *Titanic*), it took the Chinese, not known for their staunch copyright laws, to tell the truth: If it sounds just like *Titanic*, it is *Titanic*.

While I continued to have panic attacks, I often found myself so intrigued by the spectacle surrounding me—dozens of colorfully attired children handing me flowers, break-dancing troupes diving and jumping around to our music—that my panic wasn't as severe as it had been in America. And unlike the God Bless America Tour, with its grueling pace and monotonous routine of drab hotels and chain restaurants, the tour of China consisted of short flights across stunning green mountains and wide deserts, and easygoing microbus jaunts through claustrophobic yet stunningly colorful urban landscapes. As guests of the Chinese state, we stayed in top hotels, ate our meals for free, and, thanks to the exchange rate, had endless amounts of cash. The trip felt less like work and more like a paid vacation.

With half the concerts canceled and ten other musicians to explore China with, I spent very little time with The Composer, though I did note that he was being yelled at regularly by angry-looking Chinese officials. I could never tell why they were so angry with him. I don't think he could tell either. He grew thinner over the course of the three-week tour, and because he was already too thin to begin with, his appearance became alarming. There were no crates of apples from Maine, no boxes of Cap'n Crunch. Instead, each night, all of us sat down to a Chinese-style lazy Susan table in a restaurant or hotel dining room and waiters brought out dish after dish of mysterious yet delicious food: steamed lotus, flower petals, bats (their bat wings still attached, intriguingly chewy and crunchy), crawfish, water chestnuts, cow liver soup, red bean paste with steamed buns, chicken feet, chicken stuffed with fish, hot watermelon soup, broiled insects, eggs that did not come from chickens, handmade noodles, something amazing that I can only describe as meat jello, and bowls of fish soup with fish eyeballs floating on the surface, looking at us. While The Composer and many of the musicians stuck to white rice, I ate and ate and ate. I gobbled up the chicken feet, I aimed my chopsticks right at the fish eyeball. After the three months I spent on the God Bless America Tour, eating microwaved food from Ruby Tuesday and over-fried chicken gizzards at truck stops and the sad pizzas of the rural South, I couldn't get enough Chinese food, which was fresh and light and full of interesting flavors. I gnawed on the bat wings and crunched on insects. In *The Woman Warrior*, Maxine Hong Kingston notices the number of ancient Chinese heroes who were ravenous at the table. "Big eaters win," she writes. I was no woman warrior, and I was no longer fearless enough to become a war reporter, but I could still find international adventure in a fried bird's skull.

While the Chinese government officials all seemed to share a universal distaste for The Composer—the smiling, effeminate purveyor of prerecorded concerts—they were generous hosts to the rest of us. In addition to ensuring we had delicious meals three times a day (often while filming us for local Chinese TV—*American tries famous Shanghai noodle soup for first time!*), the officials guided us on an array of adventures: a tour of a silk-making factory, a dance festival, a Mongolian prayer ceremony, a tea factory, a museum full of ancient Chinese musical bells, and several shopping malls, where the weighted American dollar enabled a continual shopping spree. There were more bizarre trips as well, including one to a real estate office where a group of businessmen tried to sell us lakefront real estate in Hangzhou. There was a disquieting trip to a circus, which, in a land with less oversight of labor practices and safety precautions, involved children ascending and descending a staircase by bouncing on their heads, their neck muscles as strong and springy as pogo sticks, the top of their heads landing on each stair with a thud, then springing from the neck to the next stair, their upside-down bodies rigidly upright in the air.

While the other musicians and I vacationed, The Composer grew desperate for the Chinese to like him. So he came up with a radical idea: The Ensemble would, for the first time ever, deviate from the usual CD track. The Composer would turn off the CD, and we would play a traditional Chinese song.

The Composer came up with this idea about an hour before we were supposed to perform for four thousand people in Lanzhou, a city in China's northwest interior. The concert was also to be nationally broadcast on televisions around China. None of us knew any traditional Chinese songs, but with quick help from one of our government officials, we decided on a simple tune called "Jasmine." We listened to a CD recording of "Jasmine" and then all ten musicians quickly got to work. Within thirty minutes we had transcribed the song onto composition paper. We scribbled furiously, breaking into teams, arranging the song into parts: strings, flute, percussion, piano. We practiced it once and then it was time for the concert to begin.

When we got to "Jasmine," The Composer turned off the CD player, and for the first time in my Ensemble career, the sound of my violin mattered. Real sound floated down from the stage and into the ears of four thousand Chinese. We didn't sound that bad, at least not to me, but then I'd never heard "Jasmine" before, a song as well-known to the Chinese as "Jingle Bells" is to Americans. But the applause for "Jasmine" was faint and short-lived—The Composer's other songs were met with thousands of Chinese yelling: *Titanic! Titanic!*

During intermission our translator explained that a television celebrity would announce each of our names to the crowd. The celebrity, a stunning woman wearing a blue, rhinestone-studded ballgown, didn't speak English, and as we repeated our names for her she became distraught. I didn't care whether she pronounced my name correctly, but it was clear that she did. As the other musicians said their names aloud, the poor woman seemed to be panicking over the task of memorizing the correct pronunciation of ten difficult English names just a few minutes before she would say them on live national television.

She came up with a solution to her problem, one that I came to think of as apt retribution for all of the concerts over the years in which The Composer had announced me as Melissa, a fitting end to the last concert I ever played in which a large audience heard the real sounds I was making on my violin. In her panic to memorize all of our names, the announcer decided to just use one name for all of us, perhaps figuring that all English names sound the same to the Chinese ear:

"On the violin: JESS-CA HI-MAY! On the flute: JESS-CA HI-MAY! On the drums: JESS-CA HI-MAY! On the piano: JESS-CA HI-MAY! On the cello: JESS-CA HI-MAY!"

God Bless America Tour 2004
Pittsburgh

The Castle of Make-Believe—yes, the one from *Mister Rogers' Neighborhood*, with towers painted Mediterranean blue with white battlements and a red trolley running through it—is covered in dust, roped off in a corner beside an ancient kitchen oink in the Pittsburgh PBS station. Over one of the archways, where King Friday XIII once made speeches, a small sign has been taped that says, LOOK. BUT PLEASE DON'T TOUCH. You are shocked by how small the castle is (it seemed so much bigger on TV). In real life, it's nothing but rickety, crumbling cardboard.

But it brings back memories you didn't even know you had until you stand only inches away from its disintegrating walls, wearing your gauzy black concert dress, a violin in your hand. You couldn't have been more than four or five years old, but you hated watching Mr. Rogers. You hated the way he spoke to you, like you were a little kid, hated it because it reminded you that you were, indeed, a little kid. "You'll have things you'll want to talk about," he sang. "I. Will. Too." You might be a little kid, but you knew you couldn't talk to people on TV. You weren't stupid. And you could never follow the bizarre plot twists in the Neighborhood of Make-Believe. Why were some people real and others puppets? Why did the puppets all sound like Mr. Rogers? Why was there a castle right next to a tree with an owl in it, and a trolley running through it all, with its fast-paced piano trolley music? And where was the trolley music coming from? Where was the piano? Was the trolley also a piano? Was that possible?

Very little about *Mister Rogers' Neighborhood* made sense to you, and you had the feeling that it was all a ruse to fool you into doing something you didn't want to do, like eat your peas or drink your milk or go to bed. Years later it will strike you that perhaps Mr. Rogers wasn't meant for you, a kid of the 1980s with wonderful real-life parents who indulged in imaginary play. Perhaps Mr. Rogers was intended for your parents themselves, kids of the 1950s. Your parents were raised by people of a sterner, more sinister generation. Your grandparents didn't indulge childhood fantasies, didn't proselytize childlike imagination. Perhaps Mr. Rogers was the dad that people of your parents' generation wished they had, a greatest generation type who, despite everything that happened during the Depression and the war, still came home singing, put on a cardigan, and played make-believe. But as an actual child in the 1980s—the alleged target audience—you didn't like Mr. Rogers. You had way cooler real-life parents, thank God.

But as you stand before the crumbling edifice of Make-Believe, your violin in your hand, all grown up, you do remember one particular episode of *Mister Rogers'*. The one where he goes to a trumpet factory. You had just turned five years old and for your birthday you had received a pink leotard with purple leg warmers and a shiny new marching baton, a girly twirly decoration that was heavy in your hands and you thought of as a sword. Mr. Rogers walked through his front door like he always did, but this time he was carrying a trumpet. You put down your sword and sat close to the TV. You wanted to see what was going on with this trumpet. Mr. Rogers tossed the instrument onto the bench where he changes his shoes. Tossed it there like it was nothing.

It turns out it *is* nothing, just a toy trumpet, not a real one. He puts it to his lips and jiggles his fingers around on the keys, but no sound comes out. And Mr. Rogers says, "I wanted very much to show you how it goes *do-to-do-to-do-to-dooo* when I blow in here, but, I'm sorry to say, that it doesn't play at all."

Well, no matter, because Mr. Rogers is on the phone with Wynton Marsalis, and Mr. Rogers is about to show you a trumpet factory, the only wonderful thing you will remember about him and his show, twenty years later.

The trumpet-making process is gorgeous and complex, the perfect union of high art and industrialization, beauty and hard work. It involves an astonishing number of people, each with his or her own job to do. The first worker cuts a sheet of brass into a circle, the second shapes the circle into a three-dimensional bell, a third makes the bell tail, a fourth spins the bell tail in a machine to mold and trim and smooth it into its proper size and shape. A fifth plugs the end of the bell tail, fills it with soapy water, and puts it into a freezer that looks just like the meat freezer your grandmother uses to store the deer carcass your grandfather shoots each fall. When the water in the bell tail is frozen, the man takes it out and bends the tailpiece like a piece of spaghetti, the frozen water keeping the brass from breaking. A sixth worker crafts the tubular innards of the trumpet while a seventh man assembles the valves. The eighth puts all the tubes together and solders them, the ninth solders on the bell piece, and Mr. Rogers intones, "You know, until you see something like this, you never realize how many pieces there are in a musical instrument."

The trumpet is now completely assembled, but it's not very shiny. So a tenth person polishes the trumpet on a fast-spinning cloth wheel, making the brass gleam. An eleventh tests the sparkling new trumpet, oils its valves and checks for air leaks. Finally, the trumpet is passed to the last person of all, a musician, who puts a mouthpiece on the finished trumpet and plays a jazzy riff. It is perfect and wonderful.

All of these people doing this complex, gorgeous work, all to produce a few notes that ring like a call from the sky. It's enough to make you proud to be a member of the human race, a civilization that could think up such a wonderful process, a process with no value at its end other than the pleasure that sound brings to the human ear. If there is a true definition of *making a living*, this is it.

That's what you remember as you stare at the crumbling Castle of Make-Believe, its creator dead and gone, its puppets silent. Not the imaginary stuff, but the real assembly line of that glorious trumpet factory. The first miraculous cries of the newborn trumpet.

What you don't remember is this: After the trumpet factory tour, as Mr. Rogers feeds his fish, he talks about music in general. He says, "There are many different ways to make music," and he imitates each one: "Blowing, plucking . . . striking on a drum."

He finishes feeding the fish and continues, "But *playing about* something is a really good way to begin to do the real thing. If it's something that you're *very* interested in."

He continues: "In fact, when I was a little boy, I used to play that I was a songwriter."

He sits down on the bench by the door, about to change back into his work shoes.

"I liked to pretend that I was writing them to sing to families on television." And then he adds, triumphantly, "And now here I am really doing it!"

Long after you play your last unheard note for the Ensemble, long after the God Bless America Tour of 2004 ends with a thank-you note from The Composer ("Thanks for all your hard work. Best wishes!"), you read an article about "imposter syndrome," which is defined as "the inability to internalize achievement." You are interested in imposter syndrome because you have recently gotten a new job, the first profession you've ever had that you want to keep working at for a long time. You are a professor. You teach writing.

You like being a professor. You like teaching college students specifically because college was the time in your life when you most needed help, but were least able to ask for it. Now, you observe your students closely and try to determine who is quietly drowning. Being in front of a classroom full of students doesn't give you panic attacks the way being in front of The Composer's audiences did. When you are teaching you feel relaxed, perhaps because you are focused on other people and what they need from you, perhaps because the work feels real; you see improvements in your students' writing after they do things you have taught them to do. You teach at a public university with low tuition and working-class students who are often the first in their families to go to college. When your students talk about struggling for The Money, you listen. You try to help. Above all, you try to be honest with them. You try to be hopeful, but truthful, about what they may face after graduation. The social and economic and political icebergs that can sink an entire generation, regardless of its work ethic. The joyful and miserable reckonings—financial and otherwise—of *making a living*.

Still, you sometimes feel that you are not a *real* professor, that you are merely someone who imitates professor-like behavior. Even though you have gone through all of the steps to become a professor, even though you do all the things that professors are supposed to do, the first time a student calls you "Professor Hindman" you feel the same way you did the day Becca hired you as a violinist for The Ensemble. The university has made a mistake in hiring you. There is no way you are good enough to do this job.

But after a few semesters go by, something dawns on you: Faking is pedagogy. Faking is teaching and faking is learning and faking is the way that all human beings grow, from babies faking speech to teenagers faking coolness to professors faking wisdom. You assign readings in your classes so that your students can imitate other writers, for it is in the faking of other people's writing that one learns to write. And as for you, you fake Abigail Thomas and you fake Janet Malcolm and you fake Barbara Ehrenreich and you fake Nick Flynn and you fake Mary Karr and you fake Richard Rodriguez. You even fake yourself, zipping your person into the straightjackets of various pronouns. This allows you to pretend, for a while, that you are not really writing about yourself until one day you are able to look down on the page and say, well hell, this sounds like me. It *is* me.

If faking is pedagogy, what did I learn as a fake violinist? One thing is certain: I didn't learn how to play the violin. The Composer's music was too simple, too syrupy, to lead to any vast improvements in my violin technique.

Instead, what I was putting on, in my fake violinist role, was what it would *feel like* to be an actual, real, world-class musician. What it would feel like to tour the country and the world and be greeted by thousands of adoring fans. What it would feel like to be on television. What it would feel like for the world to see me as a serious professional classical violinist.

It was only by playing make-believe that I was finally able to put my violin under my bed where it presently gathers dust and is taken out only for the weddings of friends too cheap to hire a real professional.

Faking violin stardom ultimately allowed me to return to what captivated me at four years old when I first heard Vivaldi's "Winter." It wasn't the desire to be seen as talented. It wasn't to utilize the violin as an antimisogynist prosthetic, or a ticket to the big city, or worldly success, or respect. It wasn't The Money. It was simply this: I loved a song. Playing the role of a famous, world-class violinist allowed me to return to the feeling that playing the violin doesn't require anything more than loving a song. Or anything less.

As Mr. Rogers says at the end of the trumpet factory episode, right after he explains that as a kid he pretended he was a songwriter on TV, right before he begins to sing on TV:

"It helps to play about things. It helps you to know how it really feels."

What I Like to Fantasize

I like to fantasize that my last gig with the The Composer's Ensemble was set to the soundtrack of *The Shawshank Redemption*. Who wouldn't want to imagine such a thing for a last day on the job? It's a much more suitable soundtrack for job quitting than *Titanic*. You know the music I'm talking about: The music that plays while Andy escapes through the tunnels of shit. The redemption part.

The music starts with a calm sea of violins. You look around the mall in Bridgewater, New Jersey, at the bored, polo-shirted guys selling cellular plans, at the punk girls with facial piercings folding stacks of Chinese-made denim in the clothing store. You smell pretzels and strong perfume and some other American smell you can only label as heating-duct fabric softener. You watch the faces of the customers in front of the CD table where The Composer sits, his back to you. The customers have large bodies and small feet. They sway off-beat to the music like engorged kelp, held to the sand by mere threads.

You need air.

The violins aren't calm anymore. They begin to rise up. Higher. They build a skyscraper of sound, supported by brass scaffolding.

You struggle to the surface, above the rising crescendo of notes. You swim through the food court. You flail and you grab. You reach the exit. Your ears breech the lip of the water. The cigarette-scented winter wind hits your face. French horns lead the orchestra to the climactic note. The doors to the mall close behind you, swallowing the mall sounds. You have left it behind. Left it all behind.

One thing I've learned about movie soundtracks: They make endings seem less complicated than they really are. In real life, endings are long and messy. In real life, redemptions occur only when everything else has fallen into a deep and enduring silence.

Who Is The Composer? Finale

W hat I say:
The very last time I see The Composer, he comes to pick me up in an old, beat-up car full of empty cereal boxes and granola bar wrappers. It's rumored that the Ensemble lost a large chunk of money on the China tour. The Composer is now, for the first time since I have worked for his Ensemble, booking and driving to small gigs at the mall. Not that he minds, I don't think. He wrote me an email to confirm this gig. It said, "We are going to have lots of fun!"

It is a cold Saturday morning, New York City in January. The Composer sits in his car outside my apartment building. He is not doing the velociraptor or using his whispery stage voice. For the first time since I've known him, he is acting like a normal person, just a regular guy coming to pick up an employee to do a weekend job.

We head over the George Washington Bridge to a mall in Bridgewater, New Jersey, one that isn't particularly big or glamorous, one that is sure to be empty in the post-Christmas doldrums.

After going with The Composer to China, I performed in two

other television specials, but turned down other gigs. Because I now have a debilitating psychiatric condition, I have moved back to New York City needing a job—any job—with health insurance, which, after a few months, I am able to get. I spend my weekdays in a windowless cubicle in Upper Manhattan, where I work as a secretary, a job with full benefits. It is not musical fame, it is not saving lives in the Middle East. I dress in boring black secretary slacks and fill out Excel spreadsheets and make shitty photocopies and even shittier coffee. But I have come to see the job as its own sort of success, one that I can do well despite having several panic attacks per day. My new job means nothing other than a regular paycheck, health insurance, and full tuition reimbursement should I ever want to go to graduate school. It is not the sort of job to brag about over cocktails at a young Ivy Leaguers' night. But I can go see a doctor whenever I want, and a doctor is the only way I am going to recover enough to get another job. (Needing a job with health insurance to recover enough from an illness to get another job: an American paradox.) My secretary job, I am beginning to see, is no small thing, not for people my age. For a middle-class salary, regular work hours, and basic health care have become luxury items, the millennial generation's equivalent of the sports car, the seaside vacation house, the boat.

Perhaps The Composer can sense, on this cold morning in January of 2006, that this will be the last time I'll ever work for him, the last time I'll ever see him. Perhaps he knows that I am about to become one of the many musicians who have left his Ensemble, never to be heard from again. ("This is where your circle ends," he had said at the end of the God Bless America Tour. "My circle goes on.") Whatever the reason, he begins to talk to me about his life. During the hour-long ride to New Jersey, he tells me more about himself than he has in the past four years, more than he ever revealed during a fifty-four-city tour around America, a six-city tour of China.

And it is only because he lets me in, finally, to see his real self, with his real flaws and vulnerabilities, that I will not repeat here what he told me that day. It was the only conversation I ever had with him that felt real, and because of its realness, it will remain private. What I can say is this: The most ridiculous of tics and habits of human nature—eating only Cap'n Crunch, fleeing a room several times to check to see whether one has to pee—are based in the deepest, most sincere feelings: the desire to be loved and praised. The desire to be recognized for a special talent, a reeyell gift.

But what happens in the absence of a reeyell gift? What are one's options in America, land of the exceptional, if one is born average?

It's with this private conversation, in a car, on the way to play music or something that sounds like it, that I am finally able to see The Composer not as what he does, but who he is. He's a person waging a battle I know intimately, attempting to slay Mediocrity with the sword of Work. He's a person who, like me, struggles with *life in the body*. He's a person who, like me, is afflicted with symptoms of American madness: self-denial in the service of self-aggrandizement. A malignant fear of the possibility, reality, certainty of failure.

We arrive at the mall and The Composer sets up and we begin our hours and hours of playing the same songs over and over again. People come up to The Composer and tell him it is beautiful music. That it sounds like *Titanic*. That they fucking love *Titanic*. That *Titanic* music soothes them in a way that other music does not.

For the music of *Titanic* is not just music. It's also a story, and over the course of the four years I worked for The Composer, the music and the story became one and the same. The story of *Titanic* was never really about a sinking boat. ("I know what happens at the end!" my mom called out to me one Friday night in late 1997, when I was sixteen years old and Fernando picked me up to go to the movies. "It sinks!" she yelled after us.) Yes, it sinks, and at sixteen, this seemed like the main event to me. I did not go see *Titanic* again, did not understand the national obsession over it, did not understand the newspaper articles about hordes of people going to see the movie a second, third, thirtieth time. After all, there had been plenty of great disaster movies before, some with compelling love stories and moving soundtracks.

What made *Titanic* different, I came to realize, was its frame narrative. The movie begins not with any of the main characters, but with a team of cynical submarine operators making a fake, melodramatic documentary—a public relations ploy to justify their quest for sunken treasure. But their cynicism and fakery are no match for Old-Woman-Rose. In telling her story, Old-Woman-Rose controls the disaster. It does not control her. *Titanic* is a movie that argues less for the promise of romantic love than for the idea that horrific events can, through storytelling, be contained and controlled. That even when the most unimaginable disaster strikes, there will be survivors to tell its tales.

The desire for postdisaster control was so strong in Americans during the years I worked for the Ensemble, the years 2002–2006, that even the slightest sound of a pennywhistle was soothing. It made them think of Old-Woman-Rose in her bed, just before the credits roll, strengthened their resolve to believe that even the most shocking national tragedy will evolve over time, become a story told by old women with good senses of humor, women who go on to live full lives and have the photos on their nightstands to prove it, their memories more precious than their diamonds.

And The Composer—a man who could not recognize Beethoven's Fifth Symphony, a man who did not know who John Kerry was on the eve of the 2004 election—The Composer knew this: Americans needed music that gave the illusion of control over disaster.

This is who The Composer was: A person who did not understand America's basic facts, but wholly and completely understood its deepest feelings, its most powerful fears and desires.

And I came to understand that I needed the same things, that the only way to surface from my own panic was to hope it was temporary. To hope that somewhere, in the future, was an older version of myself able to transform disasters into stories.

I look at her now, my younger self. She is working so hard at so many things. She's playing the violin underwater and wondering why no one can hear her. She has no idea why she has disaster-brain, no idea why she has lost the ability to know the most basic things about her own body. Still, she teaches me something important: In the midst of panic, something compels her to take a look around, to take note of her surroundings, to remember what she sees.

We played on the stage of a courtyard in a midscale New Jersey mall, where people watched us from the second-floor balcony, under a soaring skylight. It was a stage built for musicians like The Composer, for musicians like me, musicians who are a few notes shy of the real thing.

Hanging from the balcony above the stage, there was a painting that I gazed at while I was playing. It seemed that this particular painting could exist only in this particular place at this particular time, with The Composer's music playing underneath it. The painting depicted an American flag superimposed over some sort of catastrophic explosion in outer space. There were New York City firefighters and there were white-gowned angels, and they all seemed to be floating somewhere around the moon.

Epilogue

The Composer smiles out at me from a photo on the Internet. He is wearing a tuxedo on a world-renowned concert stage. He has his arm around Kate Winslet.

In the years since I quit playing for the Ensemble, The Composer has gone on to perform many more PBS specials and concerts in our nation's finest concert halls, many of which include the same recordings that I once played along to in front of a dead microphone. He has also recorded concerts with school children that, as far as I can tell, must be live. It appears that he has never given up his relentless work habits. His concerts continue to raise large amounts of money for PBS and charities.

In recent years there has been brief national outrage when "live" music has turned out not to be. Consider the *New York Times* article that rocketed to the "Most Emailed" list the day after President Obama's 2009 inauguration: "The Frigid Fingers Were Live, But the Music Wasn't":

> It was not precisely lip-synching, but pretty close. The somber, elegiac tones before President Obama's oath of office at the inauguration on Tuesday came from the instruments of Yo-Yo Ma, Itzhak Perlman and two colleagues. But what the

millions on the Mall and watching on television heard was in fact a recording, made two days earlier by the quartet and matched tone for tone by the musicians playing along.

And at Obama's second inauguration in 2013, Beyoncé's lip-synching of the national anthem caused an even bigger controversy, dominating the national headlines for days. Granted, the musicians at both inaugurations were playing along to their own recordings, whereas The Composer's musicians play along to recordings done by other musicians. But in my view these are all symptoms of the same contagion: the public's insistence that live music be not only live but also utterly, flawlessly perfect. Which is to demand that it be inhuman.

Learning how to play the violin—learning to listen, really listen to sound—taught me that audiences mostly listen with their eyes. It's human. Our eyes are far more developed than our ears. Evidence for this can be found in the syntax of the way we talk about live concerts. People say they are going to go "see" a concert. "See Beyoncé." "See Itzhak Perlman." "See the Cincinnati Symphony Orchestra." I don't believe in the supremacy of live performance; it's too tempting to use one's eyes, rather than one's ears, to listen.

I believe in the value of trusting one's ears and trusting one's own emotional response to music. Even if that music happens to be, or happens to sound like, the soundtrack to a movie.

Thank You, For Real

An enormous thank you to my agent, Allison Devereux, and my editor, Tom Mayer, for their aesthetic integrity, ingenious editing, and encouragement. Thanks also to Emma Hitchcock, Nneoma Amadi-obi, Erin Winseman, Nina Hnatov, Ed Klaris, Alexia Bedat, and everyone at Norton.

Thanks to those who read and believed in and helped with this project from the very beginning: Priya Swaminathan, Rachel Carter, Abigail Rabinowitz, Rachel Aviv, Alicia Oltulski, Sara Bailey Nagorski, Josh Garrett-Davis, Michelle Legro, Isankya Koddithuwakku, Brook Wilensky-Lanford, Glenn Michael Gordon, Murwarid Abdiani, Julia Sterr, and Rita Zakes Cameron.

Thanks to those who taught me how to write: Brenda Wineapple, Ann McCutchan, Bonnie Friedman, Nicole Smith, Richard Locke, Lis Harris, Patricia O'Toole, Paul Elie, Darcy Frey, Nicole Wallack, Leslie Sharpe, Mat Johnson, and Leslie Woodard. Thanks to Rebecca Fadely, Bonnie Gochenour, Sherri Jarrett, Steve Livesay, Beverly Bisbee, and the many other kindergarten to twelfth-grade teachers I had who showed up each day and taught their hearts out. Thanks also to my violin teacher, Catherine Nelson, who taught me just how difficult and beautiful it is to play for real.

Thanks to the Toulouse Dissertation Fellowship at the University of North Texas. Thanks also to New Mexico Highlands University and Northern Kentucky University. I should probably also thank Columbia University, but I think I've thanked it enough in the form of the thirty egg-children I sold to pay its undergraduate tuition.

This book took many years to write and revise. During that time, thanks for keeping me real: Hillary Stringer, Matt Davis, Chelsea Woodard, Latoya Gordon, the Mendoza family—Tony, Riley, Concha, Catherine, and Miguel—India Long, Lindsay Smith Ferrer, Margot Fitzsimmons, Kelly Moffett, Andy Miller, Steve Leigh, Emily Detmer-Goebel, John Alberti, Kris Yohe, Kimberly Gelbwasser, Tracey Bonner, Lynn Moulton, Lorena Marques, Katie and Greg Mercer, Helen Blythe, Nathan De Lee, Jeannie Hindman, Ellery Hindman, and Donna Woodford-Gormley and son, Carl.

Thanks to Philip Glass, whose violin concertos and soundtracks inspired late-night writing sessions, and to the writers named in the book who taught me what to do.

A heap of gratitude to Edith Yokely, Angela Palm, and Justin St. Germain. Thanks also to Sergei Kogut, Joel Resnicow, and Julie Bruins.

Thank you to the person known in this book as The Composer.

Above all, my gratitude and love to my parents, Don Hindman and Susan Chiccehitto, for always, always getting me over the mountains. And my brothers, Andrew and Alex, for coming along for the ride.